Am I Crazy,
Or Is It My Shrink?

Am I Crazy, Or Is It My Shrink?

LARRY E. BEUTLER, Ph.D.,

BRUCE BONGAR, Ph.D.,

AND

JOEL N. SHURKIN

New York   Oxford

OXFORD UNIVERSITY PRESS

1998

Oxford University Press

Oxford New York
Athens Auckland Bangkok Bogotá Bombay
Buenos Aires Calcutta Cape Town Dar es Salaam
Delhi Florence Hong Kong Istanbul Karachi
Kuala Lumpur Madras Madrid Melbourne
Mexico City Nairobi Paris Singapore
Taipai Tokyo Toronto Warsaw
and associated companies in
Berlin Ibadan

Published by Oxford University Press, Inc.
198 Madison Avenue, New York, New York 10016

Oxford is registered trademark of Oxford University Press

Beutler, Larry E.
Am I crazy, or is it my shrink? / Larry E. Beutler, Bruce
Bongar, and Joel N. Shurkin.
p. cm.
Includes bibliographical references and index.
ISBN 0-19-510780-2 (cloth)
1. Psychotherapy—Popular works.   2. Consumer education.
I. Bongar, Bruce Michael.   II. Shurkin, Joel N., 1938– .
III. Title.
RC480.515.B48   1998
616.89'14—dc21   97-43546

1 3 5 7 9 8 6 4 2
Printed in the United States of America
on acid-free paper

Dedicated to our patients, in hope that they
will accept our mistakes, and in appreciation for their
patience while we have tried to learn.
—LEB and BB

For my children, Jon, Mike, and Hannah, with love.
—JNS

Contents

Acknowledgments, ix

Introduction, 3

1. What You Should Know About Therapy, 11
2. Who Offers Help and Does It Make a Difference? 29
3. How Treatment Is Kept Accountable, 45
4. Seeking the Healing Patient–Therapist Relationship, 63
5. How Helpful Is Diagnosis? 79
6. What Is Different About Different Therapies? 97
7. How We Discover What Works, 119
8. What Works with What Problems? 135
9. Am I Crazy, Or Is It My Shrink? 181

Appendix, 197

Suggested Readings, 199

Index, 205

Acknowledgments

We would like to express our appreciation to our editor Joan Bossert, and the people at Oxford University Press for bearing with us and encouraging us to begin and complete this book. They provided both the encouragement for our idea and the necessary suggestions to help us do some of the needed library research. There have been many others, as well, to whom we owe thanks—students, former students, family members, colleagues, patients, and friends who must remain nameless for lack of space.

This experience has been an interesting one. Two of us (Beutler and Bongar) have written extensively for professional audiences, but never quite thought we knew how to express ourselves to a non-professional one. With Joan Bossert's encouragement, we were able to collaborate with Joel N. Shurkin and the relationship has been a rewarding one.

LEB
BB
JNS

Am I Crazy,
Or Is It My Shrink?

Introduction

A patient sat in my office. Fifty-three years old, she is a veteran of our outpatient clinic, having come there for the last seven years. I am seeing her for the first time.

Every July 1, a new crop of psychiatry and psychology students enters the clinic and an old group of graduates moves out into practice after their seven years of postgraduate training. As the Director of Outpatient Services, I [LB] was personally evaluating all patients being transferred to new therapists at the beginning of a new training year and was interested in Mrs. T because her medical record showed no substantial symptoms of emotional disorder for six years.

Mrs. T initially entered treatment shortly after giving birth to her fourth child. The "baby blues" were more severe this time than in any previous pregnancy and it got so bad just before she sought treatment that some days she could not get herself out of bed. One day, she began to hear voices telling her to kill herself and the baby, she felt worthless, and the voices said that she should be punished for her mother's unhappiness. She was frightened and decided to seek help.

The first therapist she saw in the clinic was a third-year psychiatry resident, a young man completing his training and about to enter practice as a full-fledged psychiatrist. He saw her in psychotherapy on a weekly schedule, talking with her about her feelings of motherhood, and started her on a medication, the name of which she could no longer remember.

Mrs. T noticed some real improvement within a short time. The voices went away after a few weeks and she began feeling better. By the end of three months of treatment, she was much better. By then, however, the young psychiatrist, on whom she had become dependent, told her he was leaving. His training was ending.

Mrs. T became depressed—not as depressed as she had been—but her appetite decreased and she began experiencing some difficulty sleeping. The young psychiatrist talked her into transferring to a new, first-year resident, fresh out of medical school, to help her work through her sense of abandonment.

Since that time, she has seen five other therapists. As each academic year ended, she is transferred to a new resident or clinical psychology intern.

Mrs. T tells me she has not been depressed since the original therapist left and has experienced no return of the voices. I ask why she is still coming to the clinic. She admits that she really doesn't know, but each therapist recommended that she transfer, so she imagined that if she did not, she might relapse and become depressed again. Long after she had returned to health, she was still receiving—and paying for—treatment.

At least 100 million people currently living in the United States will, at some time in their lives, experience problems in relationships, become depressed, or develop anxiety so serious that they will merit psychiatric diagnosis and would benefit from the services of a mental health professional. Twenty-eight percent of the U.S. population (more than 70 million people) will have such problems in any given year. However only one-fourth of them will actually get treated.

Those who want treatment will seek it from psychologists, counselors, psychiatrists, social workers, nurses, family doctors, and ministers. The educations of these professionals will run from specialized training in psychology and mental health to medicine; some will have no formal training in mental health treatment at all. These professionals will come from different backgrounds, have different types of training and experience, and will use different methods.

Most of those seeking help will benefit from only a few treatment sessions; some will need and receive long-term and continuing treatment over several years. Some will feel better just by making an appointment, and will need nothing more. Some who require long-term treatment will terminate or be terminated from treatment too early and their symptoms will return. Some will get treatment that will make their lives worse, not better. Some of those who need only short-term treatment will get continuing and expensive treatment for common, ordinary problems that pass with time, and will pay for it even when support may be available from their own friends and family.

Unfortunately, many mental health practitioners don't know which patients will experience which results.

One of the saddest and most disconcerting facts facing the health care industry today is that most counselors, psychiatrists, and psychotherapists will continue to treat you as long as you are willing to come in and someone is willing to pay the bills. It is not that they are bad people or are intent on deceiving you; it is that they hear your common, ordinary problems and want to help. In so doing, they make treatment for most people more expensive and intensive than it has to be and for some, less than what is needed.

Mrs. T's experience is not uncommon. Initially, she did require treatment and sought it. She received help and it was successful. But she kept returning to the clinic out of fear of having her problem recur. She was not treated badly, but she was *unnecessarily* treated by well-meaning therapists who neither knew when to quit nor made the effort to find out if she really needed the expensive treatment she was receiving.

This book is for people who wish to seek help from mental health professionals—clinical psychologists, psychiatrists, family workers, or others in the field. We hope to educate and inform you about what therapy is, how it works, how to know when it isn't working, and when it's best to move on.

At times, you will find that we are critical of some practices of the mental health establishment, especially of psychotherapy and psychotherapists, so we must emphasize at the outset that we are both practitioners of and believers in psychotherapy. When we criticize our profession, we criticize ourselves.

As scientists and practitioners, we want to make the field better by underlining some of the abuses and the ignorance that causes patients to be mistreated. You have probably heard of people being treated in frankly unethical ways by unscrupulous psychotherapists. Indeed, these practices have occurred and we will report incidences in this book. But, in some ways, these extreme examples are the easiest to deal with and are not the most typical instances of failure. This unethical behavior (such as having sex with patients or becoming emotionally abusive to them) is easier to spot than the more frequent and usual case of the patient who must suffer a clinician's ignorance. With an incompetent therapist, you don't feel helped and you don't know if that is usual or unusual. Should I change therapists? Am I to blame? Should I tough it out? Should I give up on treatment altogether? We will try to answer these important and difficult questions.

In other words, *am I crazy, or is it my shrink?*

This book is designed to help you answer that question, regardless of whether you are being treated in a grossly neglectful and improper way or if you are receiving technically competent but ineffective treatment.

As clinical psychologists and psychotherapists, we [LB, BB] have spent a collective total of nearly forty years in the professional practice of psychotherapy and in research on its effectiveness. We have directly treated thousands of patients and consulted with our colleagues about countless others. Many of these patients have been helped by therapy, but some have not, and a few have even gotten worse despite treatment.

The public is often unaware that for most practitioners of psychotherapy, there is no Hippocratic oath—the oath that physicians take to "Do No Harm." And under certain circumstances, the courts support and protect both medical and nonmedical practitioners' use of ineffective or even dangerous procedures. There are many reasons for this state of affairs, and we will talk about some of them, but none are sufficient justification for those instances in which patients are the losers.

Like many practitioners of therapy, we worry when our patients, or those about whom we have been consulted, fail to benefit from treatment. We especially worry when we see people who get worse in spite of efforts on their behalf.

Suicide is one of the few fatal consequences of a psychiatric condition. It is also the most common emergency in psychotherapeutic practice, and the most stressful for clinicians to deal with. The first time one of us [LB] had a patient commit suicide it was a devastating experience. The woman was an inpatient in a private psychiatric hospital where I was employed. It was my first job and she was one of the first patients for whom I had primary treatment responsibilities. She was admitted after a very serious suicide attempt. We worked together for about three months and met daily on the ward or in my office. She seemed to respond well.

But then I got a job offer that seemed ideal and felt I could not turn it down. In a scenario that was not unlike that of Mrs. T, when I informed her that I'd be leaving in two months, she reacted strongly, even though she was scheduled for discharge within a few weeks. Unlike Mrs. T, however, this patient's condition deteriorated rapidly, requiring that her discharge be delayed. She went home about a month after I left, but continued to call me about once a month for the next six months. Then I did not hear from her for several months.

One morning her husband called to tell me that she had climbed into the bathtub and shot herself in the head. There followed a time of serious self-doubt, during which I questioned my suitability for this profession, and suffered substantial depression.

While this scenario is not uncommon for practicing mental health clinicians (more than 20 percent of psychologists and over 50 percent of psychiatrists will lose a patient to suicide at some time during their career), therapists often react to the loss, as I did, as if they had just lost a close friend or family member in a sudden and unexpected accident. Clearly, Freud's description of psychotherapy as the "impossible profession" is true in many ways, and reflects what one researcher, Ray London, also noted in his study of psychotherapists: For many, it is also a lonely profession.

Most of us really do care!

We both [LB, BB] elected careers as what the profession refers to as "scientist/practitioners" so that we could not only practice what we learn with our patients but could teach these skills to others and do research that would improve our work. Between us, we have been associated with five major university-affiliated medical schools. We have also been employed as professors and instructors in graduate and undergraduate departments of psychology in eight major universities and colleges. We have worked in, directed, and supervised the treatment of patients in academic departments of psychiatry, medicine, pediatrics, family practice, urology, oncology, psychology, education, and cardiovascular medicine.

At the same time, our research responsibilities and interests have made it possible for us to address the concerns raised about the professional practices of psychology, carrying out research on how effective various forms of psychotherapy are. We have had the opportunity of taking our clinical observations and problems and using them to find ways of improving both our own and others' practices.

Our research has been devoted to finding increasingly effective treatments, testing new theories and models of emotional change, and searching for a better understanding of why people have difficulties and what they can do about them. We have written over a dozen books and several hundred papers and chapters on these topics, all aimed at our professional colleagues.

But these efforts have ignored an important ingredient in the mental health equation—the needs of the patient. If we look at factors contributing to the success of treatments, we find that it is not the clinician or treatment procedure that is key, but the motivation, awareness, expectations, and preparation of the patient or client. While this is true, therapists must take responsibility for ensuring that patients become motivated, educated, and receptive to treatment.

Many books suggest how people can help themselves, what works, and how they can change their lives. The promises from these books range all the way from better sex lives to wealth and fame. We don't know if these books live up to their promises, but we think that insufficient attention has been paid to helping patients prepare themselves for treatment and providing them with enough information so they can evaluate whether they are getting the best possible treatment for their particular problems.

We hope this book will help you know when therapy is doing good, and more important, when it is doing harm. You will also learn when it is time to try a different treatment, a different therapist, or an alternative that doesn't include psychotherapy.

1

∾

What You Should Know
About Therapy

Few would question the observation that psychiatric diagnosis and treatment are imprecise arts. Few know just how imprecise, however.

One of us [BB] remembers the case of Solomon Rubin, a sixty-year-old Holocaust survivor. One day, Rubin's car was rammed by a supermarket delivery truck and was crushed against a wall. Luckily, he survived without major injuries, but from that moment he refused to get into a car, much less drive one. He knew he needed help, but instead of talking to his son, a clinical psychologist, he went to a Los Angeles psychoanalyst, who assumed, because of Rubin's past, that he suffered from survivor's guilt, a common phenomenon among those who lived through the Nazi horror. The analyst's solution: many months of "deep" psychoanalysis and a therapy that focused on exploring the memories of his youth and survival at Bergen-Belsen. Then his son found out.

The son sent him to BB, who began the usual behavioral treatments associated with such phobic conditions. After completing several weeks of treatment called systematic desensitization, Rubin, as homework assignment, began driving on short trips: a few blocks the first week, a quarter mile the second, and so on. He was told not to rush things.

11

All went beautifully for seven weeks until Rubin called BB in Los Angeles to apologize for not following his instructions properly. He had gone for a short drive on the freeway and wanted to keep going.

He was calling from Las Vegas.

Rubin spent a few more weeks making sure the therapy continued to work—it did—and he was finished.

If Rubin did suffer from survivor guilt, that was a separate issue from the phobia that was interrupting his life, and once that was fixed, Rubin could decide if he wished to reexamine his memories. He was treated with psychoanalysis because he went to a psychoanalyst. At that time and to this date, there is no literature to support the use of psychoanalysis to treat a driving phobia. It was the wrong school of therapy for what ailed Rubin. The psychoanalyst thought his approach was the right one, that he knew what was wrong with Rubin, and, most important, that his treatment would cure Rubin of his phobia.

Considering that there are more than 400 schools of psychotherapy (actually, this figure is very conservative; it is well over a decade old), and that number is constantly increasing, it's no wonder this field is plagued by a considerable lack of consensus. Disagreements abound regarding what theories are true, the origin of psychological problems, appropriate diagnostic criteria and terminologies, the nature of treatment, or even how to judge when treatment works. Meanwhile, new diagnostic and treatment methods are being created at a dizzying pace. Where does this leave you, the consumer?

This chapter will explore some of the ways that people, including psychotherapists, attempt to understand what is true and real. We will begin by looking at the differences and relative advantages of basing our beliefs on external, objective evidence rather than anecdotal evidence and emotion.

As a reader, the first thing you should know is that the psychotherapeutic treatment you receive from a therapist depends on the beliefs and theory your doctor currently accepts as "true."

Theories are not "facts." They are only guiding philosophies that suggest both the nature and cause of the problems you are having as well as a method of treatment. For example, if your therapist believes that depression arises from a biological disease or is a "chemical imbalance," he or she likely will treat you with medications. If the therapist believes the cause rises from forgotten traumas in childhood, he or she will seek to uncover these childhood events through talking therapy. These are only theories or conceptual "models" through which your psychotherapist's observations are organized.

There are few absolute and invariant truths about what causes a person to feel bad or act inappropriately. The same feeling and behavior may have very different causes for different individuals, or for the same person on different occasions, and most causes are both multifaceted and unknowable with our present methods.

While those who practice medicine, law, and even the construction trades are all guided by their particular theories, the role of theory is a bit different in the mental health community. In this field, treatment is more closely governed by the therapist's theory than the patient's problems. If the therapist believes that problems come from repressed childhood experiences and memories, all problems will be treated by trying to uncover these memories. If the therapist believes that depression is a chemical imbalance, all will probably receive medication. It is only a modest overstatement to say that each therapist offers a treatment that is consistent with the therapist's theory, regardless of what the patient's problem is.

In essence, it is a one-size-fits-all shopping experience for the unknowing psychotherapy patient. If the practice of medicine was conducted like that of psychotherapy, then doctors who specialized in obstetrics would treat headaches and appendicitis the same way they treat pregnancy, and a neurosurgeon would do brain scans and brain surgery on those with a bad back.

Suppose you are depressed and have sought help from a therapist. After six sessions, things are going badly. You don't feel any better, you don't like the therapist and you tell him so, and even suggest that you want to quit treatment. A therapist whose theory dictates that your emotional problems are caused by ineffective defenses constructed so that you do not face your problems and make changes in your life will interpret your dissatisfaction as an indication that you need more frequent treatment sessions to overcome this resistance. Your therapist may explain that things get worse before they get better and that it is good for you to face your problems. A regular Catch-22.

If your stockbroker recommended such a course, you'd be a lot more suspicious.

Alternatively, a therapist who believes that the primary healing force for depression is the power of a compatible and mutually enjoyed relationship between you and a "healer" may suggest that another therapist might better fit your style of relating and may even help you make the transition to a new therapist. In these two cases, you still have the same problem and symptoms. *You* remain the constant, the therapy becomes the variable.

Different theories lead to different courses of treatment and different reactions from the people being treated. No theory will work for all individuals and all problems. A theory may suggest recommendations that are well founded, but some theories are simply bunk.

Therapists offer varying suggestions because they have adopted beliefs from their mentors and colleagues about what makes people get better. But they usually fail to question these assumptions, regarding them as self-evident truths and applying them to everyone who walks through the door. Sometimes they fit, but sometimes—probably between 30 and 50 percent of the time—they don't.

Central to our quest of helping you recognize when you are getting the right treatment is defining the quality or validity of the knowledge you are likely to get through different avenues. In other words, what type of evidence can you trust when you make these decisions?

- Can you trust your own feelings about how you're doing?
- Can you trust your own assessment of what treatment should be accomplishing in your case?
- Are there other sources of knowledge that will help you?
- When are therapists making their recommendations based on truly valid treatments, and when are they blindly following one or another of their favored but unproven philosophies?

Yet, to be honest, there are times when therapists don't have the answers for working with certain clinical problems. Sometimes no hard and valid evidence exists for what particular treatment will serve you best.

The practice of psychotherapy has two basic avenues for judging whether certain assumptions and practices are true and valid. This is true for you and also for your psychotherapist. One of these avenues is your own personal experiences or, more precisely, the interpretations and meanings you assign to those experiences. Your personal experiences and memories of past events mold your beliefs about how and why people function and change. The result is an implied and usually unquestioned set of beliefs about what is true and what is not. Psychologists call this set of assumptions and beliefs *implicit* knowledge, because the basis of your knowledge is implied and internal instead of explicit and observable.

The second avenue to knowledge is sound scientific research. Research findings result in *empirical* knowledge—meaning that it has been tested, is observable, and can be repeated with the same results (replicable)—the basic criteria of accepting information as factual in science.

While both methods are widely used, and have serious limitations, most people put more faith in their own experience than any empirical proof revealed through scientific research. A recent TV commercial for a popular, nonprescription pain killer illustrates this fact. The charming and sincere actor asserts his belief in the effectiveness of the medication, saying: "Did I review the clinical research that proves it? No, of course not! I'm not convinced by charts and graphs. Are you? I had a headache—I tried it. That's the only kind of research that matters to me."

The lessons we learn from experience are based on memories and perceptions of events that are associated with especially strong feelings. These memories are usually remembered as stories, with the more emotional aspects playing a more central role in the events than less emotionally related elements. This is often done at the expense of accuracy. Events and memories are then linked by common, emotionally related themes. Scientists call this "anecdotal evidence." Anecdotal evidence forms the basis for most of our beliefs and has tremendous power over people's lives. There is a strong tendency for people to rely on this implicit knowledge even when better and more accurate information is available. Memories of personal experiences can easily be misinterpreted, and the beliefs themselves are remarkably fallible. Research studies have shown that even when clinicians are repeatedly shown that their anecdotal judgments are inaccurate when compared to those based on statistical formulas, when placed in a situation in which they must choose between the two, they still tend to believe in their own clinical judgments over more accurate, statistical predictions.

If we are troubled, our personal experience may be especially problematic. Sometimes what seems logical to us on the basis of anecdotal evidence simply isn't true. But this can be hard to explain to people. Throughout this book, we will provide examples of how remembered experience can lead us astray. As psychotherapists ourselves, we have found that scientific evidence, which also has its limitations, can supply us with the most accurate information and knowledge about our patients and their problems.

Personal Experience as Evidence of Whether Treatment Works

While it may be difficult to believe, our senses—even our common sense—are easily fooled. You have probably seen optical illusions, lines that seem the same size but aren't, lines that seem curved but are straight. The optical illusions illustrated in any high school psychology textbook demonstrate this. But this is not just true of our senses. More complex assumptions and beliefs that we make about the world based on sensory and perceptual experiences can also be subject to distortions. And the context of our experience has an even more serious effect on complex beliefs than on simple perceptions.

How many times in the night have you woken up, believing you hear voices? Most of us have. But if we base our lives on the anticipation or avoidance of these voices, our lives would be disrupted and rapidly become unmanageable. As the situation passes, so does our fear. Life returns to normal. We think of our fearful reaction the next morning and laugh. It was only a dream.

But what if our fears do not match our experience?

Most of us have had a momentary experience of hyperventilation and heart palpitation that has made us afraid we are having a heart attack or maybe even dying. This fear is unjustified, but not illogical, and it generally passes. But what if it doesn't? Some people become so preoccupied and consumed by such experiences that every change in breathing, every momentary experience of vertigo, every stomach or head pain, seems a shadow of disease, the closing footsteps of mortality.

It's not easy overcoming the tendency to believe in your own experiences. Ancient peoples were convinced that the world was flat because their senses could not detect any curvature on the horizon. But we don't need to find examples in ancient times. Ever watch a Boeing 747 take off? Common logic based only on our senses would never tell us that an object that large and that heavy could ever fly. Nor is it obvious to our senses that microscopic organisms cause disease, or that sex causes babies. All this knowledge came from the rudimentary application of science—the art of systematic and objective observation.

Our personal experiences also rely on our memories, which are in a constant state of flux. With each new experience, our past histories, in a sense, become rewritten, reshuffled. One of us recently wrote a brief history of his early life for his children, but a short time later discovered a description of the same events recounted by his father. The differences were remarkable. According to the father's account, things believed by the son as his own experience actually happened to his sister. Another event was something that happened to the father as a boy—adopted by the son through elusive processes, apparently linked by his desire to identify with his father. The stories had been told and retold so many times they became co-opted by the son.

Former President Ronald Reagan serves as another example of this phenomenon. On several occasions, he told people of his experiences during the liberation of concentration camps in World War II. But Reagan never left the Hal Roach Training Studio in Los Angeles where he made training films during the war. He had begun to believe his own movies.

It is a struggle to give up a memory that seems so real, especially when it is central to our identity.

Our thinking is also affected by whether we suffer from depression or another mental disorder. For example, depression-prone individuals tend to be more likely than nondepressed individuals to attribute the cause of bad events to their own defects and unchangeable personal weaknesses rather than to situations, temporary events, or correctable problems. They tend to believe and remember bad events more clearly and more often than good ones. Decades after the event, they can remember insults, slights, inconveniences, disappointments, crises—in minute, agonizing detail. Consequently, depressed people are often unduly pessimistic, have low self-esteem, and give up quickly.

In contrast, less depressed individuals tend to have clearer memories of good events than bad ones. For these individuals, the fallible, biased, and changeable nature of how they remember and perceive events can lead to erroneous conclusions about how helpful a treatment is and may have disastrous consequences for those in psychotherapy. A couple of examples from recent headlines may help us make our point.

In 1994, John Hagelin, a Harvard physicist,* announced an experiment designed to reduce violence in Washington, D.C. The Institute of Science, Technology, and Public Policy, an organization comprised of believers in the Maharishi Mahash Yogi (organizer of the Transcendental Meditation movement), would conduct an experiment in which 1,000 of their leaders would meditate in unison. Hagelin promised that this would generate a powerful anti-violence field that not only would reduce crime by spreading tranquillity, but would also make President Clinton more effective in running the country.

Hagelin declared the experiment a complete success, even though systematic tabulations of incidents of crime and violence showed clear increases during the time of the experiment. Hagelin and his fellow researchers explained these facts away, asserting that the violence rate would have been even higher without the meditation! Their belief was so great that they proposed the federal government give them a $5 million grant to continue the experiment. They didn't get it, but they did manage to illustrate how strong one's reliance

---

*Dr. Hagelin may be better known as the Nature Law Party candidate for President of the United States in the 1996 elections.

can be on anecdotal evidence, and how far removed it might be from reality.

More dramatically, late in 1995, the Public Broadcasting System presented an exposé on satanic abuse therapy. In the 1980s and early 1990s, a number of psychotherapists became convinced that specific symptoms could indicate whether someone had been subjected to sexual abuse and reprogramming by satanic cults. Their beliefs became so strong that they sought evidence to justify them, and were convinced that certain family trees were replete with illicit international alliances among covens of witches, maintained through a conspiracy over the centuries. They believed that members were recruited to these covens by parents preprogrammed not to remember their involvement in the satanic cults. These recruits were then sexually and satanically abused, indoctrinated to murder enemies of the coven, and then trained to forget that any such programming and abuse had happened, until they could pass the rituals on to their own children.

On the strength of these beliefs—their theories—these well-meaning practitioners designed extensive, expensive, and life-consuming treatments to purge the evil and reveal the hidden programming. These treatments were conducted in legitimate medical centers and clinics. Patients were subjected to "deprogramming" sessions, hypnosis, group confrontation, the withholding of social acceptance, isolation, physical restraint, the use of psychoactive medication, and other procedures intended to get them to admit their histories of abuse and satanic worship and reveal their plans to murder or abuse others.

These events probably seem incredible to you. They astound us. The presence of a hidden and secret society, unknown even to its own members, that transmitted curses and witchery over centuries without discovery stretches the boundaries of logic and probability—unless you are Steven King or Ann Rice.

Our astonishment does not mean we do not believe childhood abuse is a serious problem or that it does not happen. It *is* terrible and it *does* happen. But trivializing it or perverting it with wild conspiracy theories doesn't help the children who need our attention.

Any belief whose evidence of truth rests solely or partially on statements that sound something like these should be seriously questioned:

- It is true because important people believe it.
- It is true but only those who believe will be able to understand the proofs.
- It is true because those who have been converted attest to it.
- It is true because it produces good results.
- It is true because it exists.

The last proof is referred to as circular reasoning and is prevalent in many areas including the mental health field.

The PBS program included reports of what frequently happens in groups whose belief systems rely on such faulty evidence. The program presented ex-patients who described how they had become convinced that they had, in truth, been satanically and sexually abused. They told how they were programmed to kill members of their families and then forget their acts, even though on later reflection they acknowledged no such experiences had ever happened. Imagine the dilemma—if you can't remember it happening, it is evidence that you have been programmed to forget; if you can remember it, it is evidence that you were programmed to do it. The logic is unassailable—if you believe. But it is a classic example of circular reasoning. The proof and the symptoms are inseparable.

More important, the program documented the consequences of raising questions about the legitimacy of the treatment. Nursing staff who questioned the assumptions of treatment were disciplined, discharged, or demoted. Patients who questioned their treatment were found to be "resistant," and sometimes were confined or restrained to their beds by heavy leather straps for several days at a time, until they confessed or "remembered" that the satanic experiences had "actually happened." People once treated witches this way, often torturing them until they "confessed" their witchery. But this was contemporary America.

In a similar fashion, it has become evident that some psychotherapists believe so firmly that certain symptoms invariably mean the occurrence of a traumatic past event (circular reasoning) that, even when the patient has no recollection of such an event, therapy is focused on "uncovering" these "repressed" memories. Again, this is particularly true of sexual abuse believed to have been endured during childhood. (And again, we are not dismissing the very real and very serious problem of sexual abuse.)

One survey found that 30 percent of psychotherapists believe certain, inevitable symptoms identify the presence of repressed memories. But the specific symptoms are not consistent from therapist to therapist. In fact, different psychotherapists put their faith in different symptoms as the supposedly infallible markers of abuse. Virtually every conceivable symptom of emotional distress has been declared by someone as being an indicator of repressed memories of sexual abuse. Headaches, vague uneasiness, fears of heights or open spaces, sexual anxiety, depression, bad dreams, loss of weight, weight gain, suicidal thoughts, feelings of despair, low self-esteem, loss of sexual interest, and heightened sexual interest, as well as many more symptoms—each was identified by one therapist or another. These therapists indicated that if their chosen symptom was present, they would use whatever means necessary to uncover the memory of the abuse—and would encourage a patient to bring legal action against the perpetrators of the abuse, even without any physical corroborating evidence.

Effective psychotherapy does not require you to be a passive receptacle of the therapist's influence. Psychotherapy is an opportunity for exploration, and all assumptions are open to question—yours and the therapist's. Indeed, a "good patient" is one who keeps questioning and contrasting his or her beliefs with those offered by the therapist.

A core guideline to keep in mind when trying to determine if something is factual is whether there is any evidence—independent of your feelings—that corroborates your interpretation of events in your life. For example, it is often instructive to recall a favorite event in your childhood and then to take your parents, brothers, and sisters aside and ask them individually to describe the events you've selected as they remember them. You'll find that their reports vary widely about several important details. Consistency from multiple perspectives is not a guarantee that some observation is accurate, but it is clear that the lack of consistency should lead you to doubt the accuracy of a reported event, memory, or fact. An observation cannot be factually correct if those who have observed it in operation cannot agree on what they observed.

Scientific Research as Evidence of Whether Treatment Works

Science assumes that if a belief is valid, its consequences can be replicated or reproduced in nearly identical fashion across occasions, circumstances, or people, and that the phenomena being observed can be recorded independent of their consequences. The entire scientific method is designed to ensure that the conditions of replicability and objectivity are present. In contrast, anecdotal evidence, by its very nature, is inconsistent. Basing your life and decisions on anecdotal evidence means ignoring facts when these facts contradict your beliefs.

Depressed persons may reject the consistent reassurances of a friend that they are lovable and capable. By denying the importance of other opinions, they doom themselves to their own distorted view of the world, and their own bad feelings. They reject important information about themselves that might help them cope with their problems.

How do you approach a problem with your therapist? A place to begin your quest of discovering awareness is to ask yourself and your therapist a series of questions. Is this explanation of your problem any better than some other one? Would another explanation make equal sense for the presence of this symptom, or could any other set of events lead to your symptom? If the answer to any of these questions is "Yes," then you must question your assumptions, leaving open the possibility that more evidence may overturn your beliefs.

In the case of suspected childhood abuse, for example, does anyone in the family agree that the abuse occurred? Are there any hospital, legal, or clinical records to indicate that traumas of which you are not aware might have occurred? Has the supposed abuser been in any trouble of a similar sort? Do those other acts follow patterns usually associated with this type of offense?

In the specific case of childhood sexual assault, it is unlikely that a given perpetrator offended only one child, did it only on one occasion, or did not have other, independently observed psychiatric problems as well.

Scientific evidence has been most useful in determining what types of treatment are effective for specific problems. For more than four decades, scientists have made psychotherapy their topic of inquiry, and in that time we've learned a great deal about what works and what doesn't. But, as we said earlier, most psychotherapists operate according to theories or models that have not been validated. The effectiveness of their methods relies on their skill with common or nonspecific interventions. These interventions are methods of influence that can be present in any social relationship (things such as kindness, emotional support, encouragement), and are not the specialized components of mental health treatment. Nonspecific interventions are inherently healing, but they do not require particular expertise or academic knowledge to implement.

A benevolent, sympathetic, and sensitive therapist can do a great deal. But the best outcome for the most serious problems calls for a practical knowledge of scientifically proven procedures. Unfortunately, therapists are not legally bound either to practice effective interventions or inform patients if they are practicing scientifically credible procedures. Historically, the proofs of various viewpoints have been left for the various factions to fight about—hence, the proliferation of hundreds of different theories of psychotherapy.

Truth is not likely to emerge by an adversarial process. That doesn't work well in the courtroom and it doesn't work well in the therapist's office either. One alternative to giving in to the might-makes-right doctrine began in the courts. In legal cases involving psychotherapeutic malpractice, the court has instituted the so-called respectable minority doctrine. The law always has been troubled by the fact that while a number of professional organizations have tried to establish diagnostic and treatment standards, none of these efforts enjoys widespread acceptance within the mental health profession. As a result, the courts have taken on the task of setting the standards of acceptable practice because the profession cannot or will not.

The respectable minority rule holds that where there are disputes based on differences in theoretical approaches and methods of practice that cannot be settled by law, the clinician should be judged according to the school he or she professes to follow. This "school" must be one with definite principles, and it must be the line of thought of a "respectable minority" of the profession. Unfortunately, among the professions that practice psychotherapy, there are hundreds of "respectable minorities."

Another effort to ensure that treatments offered in mental health met minimal scientific standards was initiated with the professions of psychiatry and psychology in the middle 1980s. At the time, a group of psychiatrists and psychologists attempted to initiate federal legislation that would establish a board of review for psychotherapy. This board would have the responsibility of assessing the status of scientific evidence for different types and procedures of psychotherapy, much as the FDA is designed to do for drugs and medical equipment. Although it was a good idea, it was never accepted because of concern for costs that could or would not be borne by the government.

More recently, the Division of Clinical Psychology of the American Psychological Association (APA) commissioned a Task Force to review all different models of psychotherapy and assess the degree to which they were supported by the presence of adequate scientific evidence and whether they actually had benefits.

So scientific research has been successful in defining some treatments that work and some that don't, and a great many have been identified about which we have no knowledge of effectiveness.

We've also learned a great deal about what characteristics of therapists make them effective, even beyond—and more important than—the type of therapy they practice; what types of problems are effectively treated and which are not; what characteristics or attributes of patients bode well for good outcomes; and what the limits and strengths of our current diagnosis and treatment methods are for helping people like you. In other words, what can you legitimately expect in time, effort, and outcomes?

If scientific research has provided so much, you may wonder why you have not heard very much about it and why so few practitioners tend to rely on it. There are several reasons. For example, by its nature, empirical knowledge—that arising from scientific findings— is conservative. It takes time to conduct research, and the standard of evidence is designed to err in the direction of understating the effectiveness of procedures. This is true for medical research, as well as mental health research. In contrast, our personal knowledge of the world and our experience are liberal in their interpretations. We're quick to accept things that make sense, even if they're wrong. We err in the direction of being overinclusive rather than underinclusive. This human tendency accounts for the rumors of effective treatments and even "cures" being withheld from the public by the FDA.

It is not that these cures and treatments are withheld; it is that the scientific standard of truth accepted by the FDA (and by science generally) requires more than one supportive scientific study and specifies the nature of the research design that is acceptable. The results of a single study may be reported and accepted by the general public long before they can be validated by an independent research team, a requirement for FDA approval. The FDA standards, moreover, often are more rigorous than those adopted in other countries, further invoking the belief that a governmental agency is able to stop the distribution of effective imported treatments.

Another, and perhaps more important factor is that people tend to trust their senses and beliefs more than they trust the opinions of others, especially when contradiction exists between these sources of information. When scientific evidence is not consistent with their personal experience, they accept the interpretations that arise from their own fallible experiences.

For example, most psychotherapists in practice today report that most patients receive and benefit from having sessions over several months. They estimate that the average number of treatment sessions given to patients in their practices and clinics is about twenty. But actual patient records report that this average is much less. Many patients who come in for a first visit never come back, and 50 percent of patients who seek mental health services receive fewer than ten visits. Therapists' perceptions of their practices are distorted by their remembered experiences with those patients who come in for longer periods of time and with whom the therapists develop the strongest attachments. Most of the mental health treatment in the United States goes to fewer than 20 percent of the people who initially seek aid.

Although therapists have a hard time accepting it, many people benefit from relatively brief interventions and seem able to achieve these benefits even from people who don't carry "doctor" in front of their names.

Mental health counselors and others with substantially less training than psychologists (Ph.D.) and psychiatrists (M.D.) can be and are very helpful to most people. In fact, it may only be those with persistent or recurrent difficulties, who have not been helped by therapists with less training, who will be uniquely in need of the levels of expertise and formal knowledge that characterize the graduate training of clinical psychologists and psychiatrists—those calling themselves "doctor."

Psychologists and, to a lesser extent, psychiatrists are usually trained in research methods and should know how to critically evaluate the validity of the procedures used in reaching scientific conclusions. This type of knowledge is reflected in the M.D. and Ph.D. degrees. Other practicing psychotherapists often aren't trained to recognize the difference between authoritative opinion and research findings.

When you seek therapy, you should be aware that most psychotherapists and counselors do not have an M.D. or Ph.D. degree. Remember, clinical psychologists do have a doctorate and psychiatrists are medical doctors and therefore M.D.s. Other therapists have an M.A. (master of arts), M.S. (master of science), M.F.C.C. (master of family and child counseling), M.S.W. (master of social work), or some similar type of degree. These master's degrees usually do not include training in reviewing or conducting research. Many psychotherapists (even some with M.D. and Ph.D. degrees) are not familiar with what constitutes sound research methods, and they tend to rely on authorities whom they respect.

A recent survey found that while most practitioners sought to find solid scientific evidence for their practices, they identified popular books and articles in organizational newsletters instead of research texts and journals as their most important personal sources of scientific information. A review of these sources, however, revealed that the authors were usually nonscientists, and neither relied on scientific evidence nor reported scientific findings accurately. Books and articles based on scientific findings tend to report and support their statements by reference to articles in scientific publications. These articles are easily recognized, for the most part, by looking at their bibliographies.

But keep in mind that there is a big difference between saying that a treatment has not been shown to be scientifically valid and declaring it to be invalid. Because the rules of science are conservative, they seldom disprove a theory. No psychotherapy theory to our knowledge has ever been abandoned because it is invalid.

There are many different types of psychotherapy and mental health treatment. But only a relatively few have even been tested. Conversely, some of the treatments that have been most successful in research studies for altering problems such as depression, sleep disturbance, and anxiety are not often practiced.

A client or potential patient who is seeking to obtain a specific form of treatment may find difficulty in doing so. This disparity reflects, in part, some very rapid changes that have occurred in the field. Many new procedures and models of psychotherapy have evolved, often since most current practitioners got their training. In addition, this disparity reflects a failure of the major professional organizations and quality control bodies to ensure that continuing education is based on good science. Few of the organizations that sponsor, approve, and tabulate continuing education requirements take the time to review the scientific standing of approved courses.

It is perfectly legitimate for a patient to ask his or her therapist to discuss and provide references about the scientific basis of the treatment being offered. In 1995, three states advanced legislation that would require psychotherapists to provide informed consent to patients, which would reveal the level of scientific evidence available for the validity of the choice of treatment. In each case, this legislation was defeated, but, good or bad, it will be back. Its mere presence signals the emerging awareness that patients are consumers and should be informed of the status of the treatments that they are receiving. In the meantime, you should ask: "What makes this treatment effective or ineffective?" You should know what some of these factors are. We now turn to these factors —the things that make psychotherapy effective beyond the therapist's own skill.

GUIDELINES TO KEEP IN MIND

We have talked about two basic avenues to knowledge: one your own personal experience, the other empirical, scientific study. Both methods are fallible. Our memories of events on which we base our beliefs, and the interpretations we give these events, are subject to change. Beliefs often rely on the persuasive powers of particularly valued or admired groups and individuals—including psychotherapists. If their logic or conclusions are faulty, then so is that of those who follow them.

If you are uncertain about the treatment you are receiving, keep these recommendations in mind:

* If a therapist suggests that any specific symptom is a sure sign of some specific and past event, whether or not it is remembered, doubt the validity of the treatment offered.
* When a therapist suggests that your resistance indicates the need for more frequent, expensive, or intensive treatment, get a second opinion.
* Always remain willing to question both your own and your therapist's perceptions. Remember: independent, external evidence is both the most conservative and the most reliable when trying to determine if something is worthy of your belief.

We close this first chapter by suggesting two essential questions for you to pose as an informed psychotherapy patient:

* Is there scientific evidence that the proposed treatment(s) will help me?
* Is my psychotherapist qualified by his or her education, training, or experience to provide these treatments?

2

—— ❧ ——

Who Offers Help
and Does It Make
a Difference?

For the second time this year, Mrs. R, who is thirty-four, has lost her job. For the past eighteen months she has been trying to pull her life together after her husband took their four children and left with another woman. She drinks too much; she has no money, no hope, no friends. She sees her choices as either suicide or one last effort to get help. Where does she go? Whom does she see?

If she goes to the typical Yellow Pages, she may find a list of approximately 135 names under "Marriage and Family Counselors"; 87 under "Social Workers"; another 97 under "Psychologists"; and 48 others under "Psychiatrists." There are also lists of "Alcohol Counselors" and a cross-reference to "Licensed Practical Nurses." Some names are on more than one list.

Each name has a slew of mystifying initials after it—Ph.D., M.F.C.C., M.S.W., Psy.D., M.D., ABPP, M.Ed., FACP, LCSW—and the list goes on.

Some therapists include their areas of specialization. One block ad indicates that the therapist specializes in "children, adolescents, adults, and the problems of aging." Apparently, this person *specializes* in everyone's problems. Another ad notes that the therapist "specializes in individual, group, and family therapy." He doesn't leave many people out either. What kind of specialty includes virtually every mode of treatment available?

Still another indicates that she is a "Certified Cognitive Therapist," whatever that means; another is a "Psychoanalyst"; others include a "Jungian Analyst," a "Training Analyst," and a graduate of the Gestalt Therapy Institute. It all is very intimidating if you don't know what the distinctions are. Should Mrs. R know something about what those labels mean before seeking help from these people? Obviously the various therapists think that these titles, labels, and designations are important for the consumer.

It might help to know these things about the therapist, but for a newcomer to mental health treatment, some of the more obvious questions aren't answered by such ads. You want to know:

- Is this person effective in treating someone like me?
- Does this person know anything about my religion or beliefs?
- Is this therapist a man or a woman?
- Can this therapist speak my language?
- Can an educated person who has a secure day job really empathize with and understand my problems?

The sad truth is that the information provided to most patients by most therapists is irrelevant for answering their most pressing questions. Advertisements often assume an unrealistic degree of knowledge on the part of prospective patients. Moreover, much of the information provided, such as the therapist's academic credentials or theoretical learning, is a poor predictor of how effective the therapist will be. More relevant information on sex, socioeconomic background, values, beliefs, and success rates is missing—especially success rates.

Perhaps this chapter would be more informative if we changed its title to a question: "How Do I Know If I Will Be Helped by the Person I Select as a Therapist?"

We wish we could give a simple answer. Actually, there is no way to be absolutely sure without trying it out. But, there are some things you can do to maximize the possibility that you will choose a therapist who can help you. This is a multiple, stage process, and some of the things you should do you are already doing by reading this book. These steps involve:

- Obtaining names of potential therapists
- Assuring yourself that these therapists are legitimate and ethical practitioners
- Informing yourself about what you can expect and about your rights
- Interviewing the selected therapist
- Taking a test ride to check how the two of you do together
- Knowing when to change therapists or seek outside consultation

Unfortunately, the first few steps will only help you eliminate people who have problems that could interfere with their effectiveness, those who are dishonest, or those who are poorly trained. It is important to eliminate these therapists, though it is unfortunate both that the existent state laws do not effectively stop such people from practicing and that so many troubled people seek to become psychotherapists themselves.

As a preface to our discussion, it is important to distinguish between finding a psychotherapist and finding help. For most people who want aid with problems, counseling or psychotherapy may work. But there are other kinds of help. Even if you choose to seek personal help through psychotherapy, a great many different psychotherapists with many different credentials and types of training are available for you to choose from. You will have to decide whether you want to see a "counselor" or a "psychotherapist." A psychologist or a psychiatrist. In the next few pages we will help you know the difference and when it matters.

You should also know that getting psychotherapy is not the only alternative. There may be other avenues of help that can be as useful, perhaps more so. Would a relaxing vacation serve you just as well? How about talking to a friend or someone in the clergy?

In this chapter we will talk about the differences that exist among psychotherapists. We will also provide you with information about how to determine when you need professional help and the type of information you may need to make a useful decision. In this process, we hope to address three of the major myths that have been present in the field of psychotherapy:

- That one therapist is about the same as another.
- That psychotherapy is psychotherapy.
- That a person with emotional problems really needs to see a psychiatrist.

Who Is a Psychotherapist?

Psychotherapists are a varied group. They differ by nature of training, demographics, theoretical orientation, and level of effectiveness. No single academic degree or credential exists that signifies training in psychotherapy. Psychotherapists can come from the disciplines of medicine, nursing, psychology, counseling, social work, religion, family studies, and many other fields.

Clinicians also differ in what they focus on and how they conduct treatment. They tend to recommend the treatment they most closely identify with. Psychoanalysts advise psychoanalysis for a disproportionately large group of patients, compared to those who can statistically be expected to benefit from it; and the same goes for behavior therapists, cognitive therapists, and the myriad of others. Unless you are certain that psychotherapy or counseling is what you want, you will probably want to pick a clinician who defines him or herself broadly. This will partially ensure that the clinician who is helping you is willing to consider a variety of different treatment options.

Determining what a clinician does is even more problematic than deciphering what kind of education they have had. Among the treatments that each one endorses, you may find that some call themselves "counselors" and others refer to their treatment as "psychotherapy." These distinctions are very rough and it is difficult to say that there really is a meaningful difference. Those who do "counseling," however, usually tend to believe that problems are a normal part of making life changes. They may call you a "client" rather than a "patient," but this is likely to provide more comfort to them than to you. They may also minimize the use or significance of diagnostic labels, preferring to view all or most of your difficulties as being more reflective of normal growth processes than of "illnesses" or "disorders." If you don't think of yourself as "ill" and see yourself as going through a rough patch, you may prefer this point of view.

Those who tend to think of their problems as "illnesses" or "addictions," in contrast, may find greater compatibility with someone who designates their treatment as including "psychotherapy." Clinicians who identify themselves as psychotherapists, rather than counselors, tend to view their work as overcoming deficits, disorders, or problems, rather than as facilitating normal growth. They may diagnose problems and "treat" those who have them. It is still impossible to tell from these designations, however, either the quality of training they have received, the amount of experience they have, or the variability of treatment options they will make available to you.

Until World War II, psychiatrists provided most of the specialized mental health treatment in the United States. But the war left many more ex-soldiers and their families grieving the losses and stresses they incurred—depressed, anxious, and dysfunctional—with too few psychiatrists to go around. Psychologists and clinical social workers picked up the slack, followed in the post-Vietnam era by nurses and a variety of counselors, under different labels and with different degrees.

Don't be fooled into believing that a degree or a professional title, in and of itself, indicates that someone knows how to perform psychotherapy. Training and experience differ widely from degree to degree, even among those with the same degree or title. Psychologists and psychiatrists are the usual "doctors" in the mental health field, but they come from different backgrounds. Psychologists hold a Ph.D. (Doctor of Philosophy) or Psy.D. (Doctor of Psychology) that connotes specialized knowledge of behavior, normal and disrupted development, research methods, and measurement of emotional state and progress. Psychiatrists hold an M.D. (Medical Doctor) or a D.O. (Doctor of Osteopathy) degree that indicates medical training, expertise in physiology and neural contributors to behavior, and the ability to prescribe medications. Social workers are designated by the degree of M.S.W. (Master in Social Work) or by membership in a group, either as LCSWs (Licensed Clinical Social Workers) or NASWs (National Association of Social Workers). Nurses have an

R.N. (Registered Nurse) or L.P.N. (Licensed Practical Nurse) degree. And counselors carry almost any set of initials you can think of, most of which identify them as having received a masters degree of some kind—M.S. (Master of Science), M.A. (Master of Arts), M.F.C.C. (Master of Family and Child Counseling), M.Ed. (Master of Education), M.B.C. (Master of Behavioral Counseling), and so on. Each state and university may use somewhat different degrees to designate this type of training.

Those with these degrees do not necessarily practice psychotherapy, and many who both have the degrees and advertise themselves as psychotherapists have had no formal training in this practice. None of the plethora of degrees provides any assurance that the clinician has been trained specifically to practice the form of psychotherapy that will be of most help to you. Some physicians holding an M.D. or D.O. degree are psychotherapists, but most are not and most have had no substantial or special training in these procedures. Likewise, psychologists hold a doctoral degree, usually a Ph.D. and sometimes a Psy.D. degree, but this is a very nonspecific designation and does not, by itself, indicate anything about their credentials for practicing psychotherapy. People also get Ph.D.s in English literature and geography, so it is important to know that a psychotherapist has a doctorate in clinical or counseling psychology.

Only in the past twenty years have states and Canadian provinces begun licensing psychologists, social workers, and counselors. Yet many states still have no way of legally accrediting nondoctoral therapists and counselors. While all states and most provinces offer licenses to those who meet certain standards as physicians and psychologists, these laws typically do not designate whether the physician is a psychiatrist or whether the psychologist is a mental health professional or a research psychologist who studies bees. Someone in Florida once successfully registered his hamster—to prove a point.

Several years ago, one of the authors was asked to consult with Florida psychologists to find ways of controlling malpractice after the state laws that required proof of credentials for psychologists were "sunsetted"—they went out of effect, having been passed for only a designated trial period. Seeing opportunities, lots of people changed professions. A plumber, an engineer, an unemployed itinerant, an ex-English teacher, and many others hung up their shingles as "psychologists," including, the author was told, the aforementioned hamster. The hamster, of course, was registered under an assumed name and with falsified credentials.

Another development began in the 1970s that also increased the disparity among individuals with similar designations or degrees. Training psychotherapists became a business. The mantra of the 1960s and 1970s was mind expansion. We saw the introduction of marijuana, LSD, and other recreational drugs among the middle classes. No longer was drug use a problem of the uneducated and the disenfranchised. Interest in the mind was popular, and psychology became, and largely has remained, the favored major among university undergraduates.

Until then, the few graduate programs that trained psychologists in Ph.D. programs were housed in major research universities. But with the growing numbers of interested students, the number of programs and student slots allotted to clinical, counseling, or school psychology was insufficient to meet the demands from graduating seniors. They all wanted to go into practice as psychotherapists. Yet fewer than 5 percent of those who applied for graduate training in clinical psychology, the largest area of professional psychology, were admitted. And in fact it is harder to get into these programs than to get into a medical school.

Universities have always allocated money as a function of how many students a department or program admits. But graduate students generated more resources than undergraduates, and those pursuing doctoral training generated more money than those pursuing master's degrees. It's no surprise, then, that universities expanded their psychology programs. Free-standing graduate schools of psychology, most not credentialed by the usual oversight bodies, sprang up all over the country, especially on the East and West coasts. These new programs often supported themselves by charging what the market would bear—and that was considerable. This market-driven situation has in the recent past changed as accrediting agencies asked tougher questions. The highest quality schools survived; the others did not (we hope).

New degrees were introduced—Psy.D., M.F.C.C., M.B.C., and so on. Even if you didn't get a college degree, you could obtain special certificates in alcohol counseling or drug abuse counseling. Soon, most of the Ph.D. and Psy.D. degrees in psychology were being offered outside a regular university, and without the benefit either of a commonly accepted curriculum or a set of training standards.

In the past two decades, we've seen some concerted efforts to increase the consistency of training standards, a process probably most successful for psychiatrists and psychologists at the doctoral levels, and for clinical social workers at the master's degree level. While wide variation still remains even among those designated by these titles and degrees, the titles have come to mean that those licensed under them at least share certain training experiences.

Unfortunately, that's fewer than half of those offering services as psychotherapists or counselors.

So much for designations. They aren't very helpful, but this is where most people, nonetheless, must start in their quest for help. The daunting task of finding a good psychotherapist through the morass of degrees and credentials is all the more difficult because even when one has special training and experience as a psychother-apist, there is no assurance that that person is any good at it. Among noted psychotherapists, some have been anthropologists, and others have not completed any formal degree in a field associated with psy-chotherapy. Housewives, college professors, and other laypeople can all be as effective as psychotherapists, at least some of the time.

In the next two chapters we will address the question of how to find a good psychotherapist in the midst of this confusion.

Will Therapy Help?

In this section, we will attempt to dispel the myth that one always needs a psychotherapist or mental health clinician with highly devel-oped skills for various problems. Treatments are as different as psy-chotherapists, and patients differ too. What's critical is whether you need a professional mental health clinician at all, and, if so, what type of therapist and treatment will be useful.

A recent survey in *Consumer Reports* revealed that the majority of those respondents who had sought psychotherapy found it helpful. You may not be surprised to know that respondents were over-whelmingly happier with the amount and quality of help they had obtained from psychotherapy than they were about the help they received from lawyers when seeking legal services. This report is consistent with most contemporary conclusions of research scientists who study psychotherapy. *Research has found that psychotherapy is effective for most people, for most problems, most of the time.* In fact, about 14 percent of those who call for an appointment begin to feel better just by making the appointment.

If you enter psychotherapy, and if you attend at least six regularly scheduled sessions, without undue cancellations, you are likely to find it helpful. Between 60 and 95 percent of those who seek help experience benefit, depending on the nature and severity of their problem.

There is a predictable pattern this help will take. If your psychotherapy is going to be successful, your first indication may occur before you actually notice any change in the feelings of anxiety or depression you've been expressing. You will probably begin to experience a sense of hopefulness, albeit somewhat tentatively at first. This is a good sign, and if you don't notice it, at least from time to time within the first six regularly scheduled sessions, it might mean that you and your therapist are not working well together.

It may not be until you've attended from fifteen to twenty sessions that you—assuming that you're the average patient—begin to really notice that you are less anxious or depressed, that your social functioning is getting a little bit better, that the problem for which you are seeking help is improving, and that you are recovering some of your lost self-confidence. Many people can quit at this point without suffering any ill consequences and with the feeling of being helped. If the problem has been recurrent and is still impairing your ability to work and relate to others, continued improvement is likely to continue for another twenty to thirty sessions. Setbacks are not uncommon and progress often is erratic, but the sessions still are giving you benefit. Of course, this is the average course of treatment for the average patient seeing the average therapist. Since so many averages are unlikely to come together at once, your circumstances may be a bit different.

At the end of one year of weekly therapy, most people find themselves relatively free from their troubling symptoms. About half of those who persevere are helped substantially by psychotherapy within a period of six months, and about 80 percent are helped within a year.

More serious problems—ones we will explain shortly—may take longer than one-time situational problems, longer than a year in some cases. There is evidence from the *Consumer Reports* survey, and other controlled research, to indicate that the longer treatment lasts, the more satisfaction and benefits increase, especially among people with many different and complex problems. Improvement rates also increase for those with complex and recurrent problems if they have sought help from trained mental health practitioners, and have friendships and social groups from whom they can obtain continuing emotional support.

If your problem is depression, the chances are very good that a given episode will pass in a period of three to four months, even without specialized help. This may be difficult to believe, but most depressive episodes are "self-limiting"—despite the feelings of hopelessness that accompany them, they almost always pass with time. The problem with depression, especially if it's associated with a change in weight or sexual interest, or disturbed sleep and declining social interests, is that it usually will come back if you don't get specialized help. Such treatment may reduce the likelihood of this "relapse," especially if your depression has been going on for three months or longer.

One of the most interesting discoveries about psychotherapy in recent years is that while short-term treatments of twenty or so weeks can often be effective for treating most people with anxiety and depression, the longer you stay in treatment, the more satisfied you will be. This satisfaction seems to be consistent across a wide variety of problems that might motivate people to seek treatment, and occurs regardless of who you go to for help.

However, the *Consumer Reports* survey revealed that therapists with a good deal of formal training as psychologists, social workers, or psychiatrists, and who worked as professional therapists in mental health settings, were more helpful and effective than physicians and lay counselors. These advanced-level professionals were also rated more effective than people trained as marriage or family counselors when treatment exceeded six months in length.

Research also indicates that you will need long-term treatment for very complex and recurrent problems, and when you have long-standing interpersonal difficulties such as repeated failures in marriage-like relationships, excessive social inhibitions, and trouble with the law.

The Patient's Role

What is interesting about psychotherapy is that much depends on you. Most of the benefit you receive is relative to your motivation to get well. In fact, in order of importance, the characteristics and skill of the therapist and the nature of the therapy are secondary considerations. To obtain the maximum help, you must be willing to work hard and be motivated to make a change in your life. A good therapist may and should motivate you even more. But you are really the key to your success.

The most important quality of a therapist is the ability to listen and care, which can't be guaranteed by formal training. In fact, formal training doesn't seem to assist a prospective therapist in developing these skills to any great degree. Therapists, as people, learned these things in their own conducive family and social environment long before they attended college. We call these general abilities of therapists the "common" or "nonspecific" contributors to treatment efficacy, and they work as much to aid the effects of medication as they do in psychotherapy.

The other important contributions to the effectiveness of therapy come from specific techniques and knowledge, things taught to mental health professionals through formal coursework and fieldwork experiences. Among the three factors that contribute to the success of therapy—patient commitment and motivation, therapist caring and support, and the technical procedures of psychotherapy—technical skills and procedures are by far the least important.

Yet many people seem to be good listeners and are helpful—neighbors, family members, friends or acquaintances, even the grocery clerk or barber, or, for that matter, psychotherapists and counselors whose backgrounds are a bit untraditional. By being good listeners, all these people may offer a therapeutic relationship.

But the more your problem interferes with your daily life, the longer it persists, the more frequently it occurs, and the less you have access to supportive family and friends, the more important these specialized skills will become.

While you may need the specialized skills of a highly trained psychotherapist or psychologist, psychotherapy is only one of the avenues for change. Symptoms of depression, over a period of two weeks or more—especially when these symptoms include what therapists call "vegetative signs"—are frequently helped by medication, at least over the short run. Vegetative signs are disturbances in appetite, sexual desires, social pleasure, energy, sleep patterns, and quality of work and interpersonal activities, all of which indicate reduced ability to get along from day to day. Medications are an important part of helping people with problems of this type and several others.

In the short run, medications are no more (and most summaries suggest that they are even less) effective than a twenty-to-thirty-session course of psychotherapy, but the effects of medications are usually faster and sometimes more dramatic than those for psychotherapy. Moreover, these effects are specific to many of the symptoms that motivate you to seek help, unlike the more general effects of psychotherapy or counseling.

However, because the results obtained from taking prescribed medications are usually quick and sometimes dramatic, patients notice them more easily than changes that are gradual, as they tend to be in psychotherapy. Because of this, the overall value of medications may be overrated by both medical doctors and patients, since they can see the effects. Yet systematic research indicates that, for many problems, the rate of relapse is much higher for those receiving drug treatments than for those receiving psychotherapy. Moreover, physicians, even psychiatrists, who often depend on literature from drug companies to keep them abreast of the field, are often unaware of this fact. As a result, medication is frequently overused, often incorrectly prescribed, and is sometimes actually dangerous.

Interestingly, much of the effectiveness of medications, at least for depression and anxiety, can be attributed to the enthusiasm of the prescribing physician and his or her ability to convince you that they will be effective.

Despite these drawbacks, a percentage (probably around 20 percent) of people who take medication for depression and anxiety will not need any other treatment. It is the other 80 percent who concern us. As a rule, if the problem affects many areas of life and continues to occur, psychotherapy may be necessary either as an alternative to medication or a supplement to it.

What Type of Psychotherapist Do I Need?

But what type of psychotherapist best fits you and your problem? Most people receiving psychotherapy will benefit from it and require no other treatment. For these people, liking the therapist outweighs the type of symptoms or the type of therapist.

A very significant minority of individuals seeking help—probably in the neighborhood of 20 percent—do not benefit from merely being exposed to a caring person. These individuals need very specific types of therapy and high levels of training, and technical proficiency may be of help to them. For example, arguably the best scientific study of long-term psychotherapy in a managed health care environment has found that most therapists are effective with most patients. But some outstanding therapists are distinguished by being both more effective than most with all patients, as well as with a larger variety of patients and problems. The value of formal training and the skill of these individuals are best and most easily seen when patient's problems are particularly severe.

The more complex and recurrent the problem, the more you need a highly specialized treatment program administered by a person with highly specialized skills and knowledge. It's the difference between going to a general practitioner in medicine or a specialist—sometimes you do need a specialist.

But what about specialized skills for different problems? While there are certainly some treatments that we can now suggest are effective even when applied by widely diverse psychotherapists, there are also certain myths about the degree of specificity of treatment needed to help people.

In our complex and heterogeneous society, many people strive to highlight their distinctiveness. It is frequently thought that you have to be an ex-alcoholic to help one; if you are a member of a special underrepresented ethnic or sexual group, that your chances for help are improved if you get help from someone just like you. Certainly, sensitivity to the uniqueness of subcultures and particular problems is helpful. Women do seem to experience different problems from men, and African Americans have different problems than Asian Americans in their daily lives. And alcoholics frequently do feel more understood by those who have had the same problem.

In addressing these issues, there is ample reason to believe that a therapist who either is similar to the patient in some important ways or is especially sensitive to and knowledgeable about these differences will be better accepted and have greater opportunity for making gains. However, despite considerable rhetoric to the contrary, there is precious little evidence that women, African Americans, Asian Americans, Hispanic Americans, or addicts need a special kind of therapy or therapist. They need what we all need—a sensitive and knowledgeable therapist who will help them confront their problems. There is little or no evidence that feminist therapy or black therapy or therapy by "alcoholics" is more effective than any of the alternatives.

Although having a therapist who shares certain views and backgrounds seems to make for a more comfortable therapeutic environment (which means you are likely to stay in treatment longer), special treatments based on ethnic and sexual differences have not proven themselves to be uniquely helpful. As always, the powers of the individual therapist can and do outweigh the effects of special theories or treatments.

GUIDELINES TO KEEP IN MIND

Like any professional activity, the nature of psychotherapy is often imbued with myths and legends. There are many myths in psychotherapy since it is a field that historically developed according to different theories. We will talk about many of these in the coming chapters.

By now we hope that we have dispelled one of the oldest and most persistent myths in our profession—the myth that all psychotherapists are essentially equal. In fact, there are wide differences among psychotherapists in training, experience, expertise, and interests. Much of the rest of this book will be devoted to illustrating that not all psychotherapies are equal, either.

Certainly, the awareness that not all are alike, that one size does not fit all, is also true when applied to patients with different problems and symptoms. Among patients with situational and stress-induced problems, most psychotherapists will probably have equivalent rates of effectiveness, regardless of training and experience. However, this is probably not true for patients whose problems are recurrent, complex, pervasive, and long-standing. Among this group of patients, not all symptoms are responsive to the same set of procedures or therapists. Thus, we offer the following recommendations:

* Most problems that are caused by a sudden change in your circumstances or living situation pass with time, especially if you have a supportive network of friends and family to help you. Your own resources and patience will do much to see you through these situational adjustments.
* If a problem is recent rather than long term, if it is the first occurrence, if it is situational rather than an enduring pattern in your behavior, and if it is more noticeable to you than to others, it may be appropriate and helpful to start the process of finding help by talking to trusted friends, family, a member of the clergy, or a family doctor (not necessarily in that order).
* Recurrent problems, or ones that are disruptive to many aspects of your life, or are determined by the accumulation of many life-changing occurrences rather than by a single event, or have been unrelenting for a month or more may need the attention of a professional therapist with specific training and technical knowledge.
* If you want to take advantage of the continuing and progressive effects of long-term treatments, you should make sure you are seeing someone who has a good deal of training and experience beyond the minimum to be a psychotherapist. If all you want is

help with your immediate problem, then issues of therapist training and experience are less important.

* While there is little evidence that a therapist who shares your
problem or who is ethnically and demographically like you will be
able to aid you more than one who is different, you may be more
comfortable and feel more understood if you see such a therapist.
Examine your own preferences, and select a therapist whose background suits you—don't be inhibited by your fear of asking. We'll
arm you with the right questions later.

3

How Treatment Is
Kept Accountable

Rex was suffering from panic attacks. They began suddenly one day while he was driving home from work. Work had been stressful, but Rex didn't think that this was much of a problem. His work was often stressful. He sought advice from his family physician who prescribed the tranquilizer Xanax and then referred him to a new psychologist who had just opened an office in the same building. Rex's doctor had recently met the psychologist and was impressed with him.

Rex began seeing Dr. J in August. But by January, he still was not feeling any better and his panic attacks were becoming more frequent. He was now afraid of driving, afraid of having a panic attack and not being able to get home, or having an accident. He began to miss work and was developing a sleeping problem. It took him a very long time to fall asleep and he frequently awoke during the night, unable to return to sleep. Some nights he didn't sleep at all.

Dr. J advanced the theory that Rex had failed to resolve some of his deep-seated anger toward his father who had run away when Rex was six and was killed in a barroom brawl seven years later. Dr. J explained that Rex had never appropriately grieved his father's death and that revisiting the relationship with his father would be necessary to stop his symptoms.

Some time later, Dr. J revealed that he had psychic powers and might be able to channel communication between Rex and his deceased father. He suggested that this might help Rex work through his conflicts with his father. Rex was skeptical, but felt like he had nothing to lose and Dr. J assured him that he had expertise in this area. There followed a series of sessions—"seances," Rex called them—in which Rex would speak to his father and Dr. J would then channel a response back. Sometimes, these exchanges seemed quite real to Rex, causing him to wonder if his father was present. However, instead of easing his anxiety, the distress associated with these sessions seemed to increase Rex's panic attacks, provoking Dr. J to assure Rex that this meant he was truly confronting his fears.

When Rex finally complained to his family doctor, he was encouraged to lodge a complaint with the State Board of Psychologist Examiners. When Rex did, he found that Dr. J had never been licensed as a psychologist in the state and was wanted in two other states for practicing without a license.

Dr. J was a fraud.

The treatment offered Rex was unusual and he was justifiably a little skeptical. But more often than not, fraudulent therapists behave much like trained and experienced ones. Some are effective, some are not. What is important is whether the treatment addresses the condition. A caring but fraudulent or untrained therapist may provide help to those who do not need the specific skills and knowledge that comes only from academic training, intensive reading, and structured practice.

Rex had a specific problem for which effective and proven treatments exist. Caring and support are helpful, but they are not sufficient to correct these problems. Moreover, the specific procedures selected and used by Dr. J were inappropriate for Rex's symptoms and some, like channeling, are not accepted methods of treatment. The focus on his father and uncovering deep-seated conflicts, with or without the channeling, was problematic. It relies on an unproven method for treating this specific symptom regardless of its origin. A therapist who is familiar with and trained in the treatment of panic would usually focus on removing the panic symptom first, and then worry later about explorations of early childhood and relationships if these were still problems.

Can you spot the ineffective or harmful therapist before you enter treatment? Probably not. But there are some things that may help protect you from the ignorant, the untrained, and the deceitful—or at least, ways to reduce the likelihood of your finding them. That is, there are systems and methods that have been instituted to make psychotherapists accountable, and at least some of these can be used to help you avoid individuals who either misrepresent their training or who have been found to be unethical and dangerous in the past.

We hope we have discouraged you from relying on the Yellow Pages. They tell us nothing that can help us avoid the fraudulent and dangerous therapist or find the effective one. Information obtained from various formal systems of accountability are only somewhat better. They can provide some assurance that the therapist is legitimate, but still do little to assure you that the therapist will be effective with you. In the next chapter, we will return to this issue of effectiveness, exploring ways to avoid therapists who use ineffective and harmful processes and procedures. Then, we will discuss what procedures work with what types of problems and people. It takes awareness of all of these components to ultimately know when your treatment is working and when it ceases to work. Knowing how to recognize the ineffective, fraudulent, and untrained therapist should help you narrow the field of therapists from which to choose, and guide you to leave a therapist who may be unskilled in treating your problem. In the process of this exploration, moreover, we hope that you will come to realize that the concept of "good treatment" is a bit more complex than you might initially think.

But, let us take things in step, beginning with the process of initially selecting a therapist and turn our attention in this chapter to describing the various systems that have been put in place by governmental and professional agencies to monitor and enforce accountability among practitioners.

We will point out that some systems for assuring accountability are frankly as problematic as the problems they are trying to solve. You should be aware of this so that you will know which avenues to pursue and which to distrust. However, as we approach this issue, we hope that neither our critique of the field nor the morass of confusion that we have described will dissuade you from the effort, because if you are successful in finding a good therapist, it can be a rewarding experience.

There have been a variety of efforts, some initiated by the mental health professions themselves and others by political and bureaucratic organizations, to monitor therapists and ensure that practitioners who offer services to the public are either qualified or effective. Initially, selecting a practitioner by accessing the information made available through these formal institutions is a way that may aid patients to weed out therapists who have not received a minimal level of training and experience.

Many avenues are available for checking a clinician's credentials, but many of these methods are clumsy and inefficient. Moreover, most do not take into account whether the practitioner either practices scientifically valid treatments or is effective. It's unfortunate but true: We can't escape the fact that we know *what* is effective but not *who*.

What Does "Effective" Mean, and How Do I Know I'm Getting Better?

On its face, it would seem simple to determine if therapists are effective. And, it shouldn't matter who is making that determination—the professional, the patient, the law, or an insurance company. However, who is deciding this question does make a difference. There are at least three very different definitions of what constitutes a valid or effective treatment—one based on making people better, one based on how expensive the service is, and one based on its popular appeal.

The most usual recommendation made to those seeking treatment is to check the professional qualifications of the provider. This procedure, many believe, is the best way to ensure that you find a practitioner likely to be effective in alleviating your problems.

So, *first, check the therapist's credentials.*

That's harder than it sounds. It involves some value judgments about the relative worth of different types of training. Sometimes, such considerations may be relevant; at other times, they are not. Moreover, the established evaluative procedures come from many different sources and do not yield the same or equivalent results. Some of these methods have been constructed by the professions themselves and others by governmental agencies.

The process of checking a clinician's credentials is well meaning, but it is based on the often dubious assumption that there is a meaningful relationship between how skilled and helpful the therapist is and the nature of the therapist's education. This relationship is present only when patient problems require specific and highly technical treatment. For most people it is not a strong relationship. But when specific technical training is called for, we need to know how to find a therapist who has it.

For example, Dr. J actually may have done well with a patient whose problem was well suited to his brand of treatment, even without training. But Rex needed a different treatment for which Dr. J was not prepared. Knowing the clinician's background helps you eliminate the untrained therapist—doing so limits the field of therapists from which to choose.

Unfortunately, the little value that many types of credential reviews provide has been lessened by the intrusion into this process by two other institutions—health system administrators and the courts. These institutions also make judgments of clinical effectiveness, usually based on different criteria than the practitioner's credentials, but they are equally problematic.

The efforts of health care systems have been to cut costs, either for the protection of the public or for their stockholders. This is a different goal from that of either the professions that practice treatment or the courts, whose task has been to adjudicate suits against practitioners. Courts have tried to define the nature of valid services in terms of their appeal to other practitioners. Professional organizations, educational institutions, health care systems, and the courts, all have different definitions of what is effective. As we will see, most of these definitions are different from what you or I would think of when we use this term.

Institutional Accountability of Clinicians

Professional Credentialing

Because the degrees, training, and activities of psychotherapists are so diverse, it is no mean task to evaluate a psychotherapist's professional credentials. We have four systems to govern the training and practice of psychotherapy.

The first is a system for *accrediting institutions,* the universities or colleges that grant degrees. These accrediting bodies established by state and federal governments indicate that the school has met certain standards in terms of faculty credentials, instruction, and facilities.

You can find out if the school from which a given clinician received training is accredited from your local public or university library. Libraries usually maintain books that list academic institutions, by state or region, and indicate regional accreditation by the relevant governmental agency.

In the United States, the U.S. Department of Education established four regional accrediting bodies. These regional accrediting bodies (the Western, Eastern, Midwestern, and Southern Associations of Schools and Colleges) pass such judgments on universities within their regions and classify them according to their missions (undergraduate teaching, research, etc.) and the types of facilities and degrees offered. Each school accredited by these bodies publishes this information, along with other approvals, in their regular catalogues.

Sometimes you will find that the school from which the clinician graduated lists none of the four regional accrediting agencies. Instead, it may note that it is accredited by a state agency (such as state board or department of education). Don't place great faith in these state organizations. They are not as consistent or as informative as credentials received from one of the four regional organizations. Some states simply maintain a listing of educational institutions rather than actually checking them.

Frequently, schools listed by the state board of higher education (or its equivalent) can offer degrees, even though the college or university has not received accreditation from the relevant regional association of schools and colleges. Even when the state designation implies an actual evaluation process, the lack of state-to-state standards makes the designation less than optimally meaningful.

The regional accreditation agencies for schools, colleges, and universities do not, however, accredit disciplines like psychotherapy, medicine, psychology, and so on. They only evaluate the institutions that offer degrees. While they may be sufficient to help a high school graduate to select a college, they are insufficient, by themselves, to provide specific information to consumers of psychotherapy. The specific programs within universities and colleges are monitored by the other systems for evaluating the quality of education.

Because of the limitations of a system that accredits only the school rather than the department or program, the professions established a second system for ensuring a program's quality. These accreditation systems, however, have no legal standing and derive their authority from professional groups themselves rather than from a governmental agency.

These self-monitoring structures identify the *programs* within regionally accredited universities that provide adequate training in a specific discipline. The American Medical Association and the affiliated group from the American Psychiatric Association designate medical schools and psychiatric residencies that meet certain standards for training in psychiatry and medicine; the Committee on Accreditation (COA), a multiprofessional group composed of representatives from the American Psychological Association, the American Psychological Society, numerous training organizations, specialty groups, and various state licensing and psychology standards groups, all evaluate and list specific schools and programs that meet certain standards for training in clinical, counseling, school, and industrial and organizational psychology. The National Association of Social Workers designates approved programs for training in psychiatric social work.

The central offices of these groups maintain lists. If the prospective therapist is a psychiatrist, physician, psychologist, nurse, or social worker, a call to the relevant professional association's central office—usually in Washington, D.C.—will reveal if the program from which the prospective therapist graduated has met standards set by their profession (see Appendix).

While these informal credentialing bodies work for the better established professions, counselors and psychotherapists who have degrees, such as M.Ed., M.F.C.C., M.A., M.S., are not represented by a single professional group or a consistent set of training standards. They are an even more diverse group than psychiatrists, psychologists, and social workers, in terms of education.

A general review of an academic institution, provided by a regional accreditation board or by a professional discipline, can be helpful in most instances—for example, it would be important to know if the therapist you are consulting is untrained or unethical. It does little to protect you from dangerous or crazy individuals who hang up a shingle.

Some therapists, either because they believe that they are being discriminated against in spite of their great gifts, or because of more malevolent motives, misrepresent themselves, their education, and their experience. State and provincial *licensing boards*, the third level of credential review, protect you against these dangers by checking and reviewing each applicant's specific credentials.

Although licensing conveys assurance of training and, within reason, assurance that one is accurately reporting information about education and training, the requirements for licensing vary widely from discipline to discipline, and from state to state.

Moreover, this legal designation of licensing does not provide either a guarantee of specialized training or—again—assurance that the therapist is any good. In most states, any licensed physician can practice psychotherapy, although few have the specific training. Similarly, a license as a psychologist does not always distinguish between one who has spent years in training to help emotionally distressed individuals and one whose professional life has been in an animal research laboratory.

Nonetheless, there are advantages of assessing a practitioner's credentials through state licensing boards. Unlike the previous two levels of credential assessment, professional licensing boards are usually state agencies that assess individual rather than university or program qualities. A prospective patient might find it informative to ask the therapist if she or he is licensed and by whom.

Because unscrupulous therapists might give false information or provide phone numbers of nongovernmental membership organizations that have a vested interest in their practice, a call to the state attorney general's office can result in a list of independent and government-run licensing boards, addresses, and phone numbers. A call or letter will reveal if the relevant state agency licenses that therapist.

The fourth system for checking a psychotherapist's credentials is through *associations* specifically set up to evaluate advanced standing and special qualifications. They try to identify "competence" along with offering assurance of minimal training. Like licensing, these groups provide individual assessment and review of credentials. Nonetheless, one should be cautious about using lists from such groups because these are membership organizations and they have no legal standing. It is not unheard of for people with inadequate training or incompetent practices to band together to create their own organization to protect their incompetence.

If you have already been assured that the academic institution and training program are legitimate, and that the therapist is licensed, then information about special affiliations may be helpful in determining the therapist's level and areas of expertise.

In psychiatry, medicine, and psychology, advanced standing in the profession is designated both by awarding of a Diplomate and being named a Fellow. Both designations reflect one's status among peers, though the latter usually comes from recognition of work on behalf of the profession rather than for professional competence. The designation as a "Diplomate" or "Board Certified" indicates that the person has passed competency examinations in an area of expertise. Someone awarded a Diplomate usually designates this status by placing the initials of the granting agency behind one's name (F.R.A.P., F.A.A.C.P., A.B.P.P., etc.). In disciplines like social work, special certification from the National Association of Social Workers (NASW) or a certificate or license (LCSW) designate special competency.

While degrees, certified programs, licenses, and professional memberships are impressive, only the award of a Diplomate indicates that the psychotherapist has achieved a predetermined level of competence. And even this is fairly general. Specialties are poorly defined in the mental health areas and they are likely to come and go with the times.

Narrative information about a potential psychotherapist is also available, usually through your public library or a local university library. The various professions maintain listings of those individuals whose credentials qualify them to work in certain areas. Psychologists may indicate their listing in the *National Register of Health Service Providers in Psychology;* psychiatrists may note their membership in the Group for the Advancement of Psychiatry, the Academy of Child and Adolescent Psychiatry, or their listing in the *Biographical Directory of the American Psychiatric Association.* These directories give specific information on types of professional activities, background, and professional interests. Your queries about such designations are appropriate and the prospective therapist should be willing to provide a list of qualifications for you. The qualifications should include both standards of formal training and state licensing.

Managed Health Care: Cost versus Accountability

The health care system—those institutions that provide coverage and pay for treatment—also is concerned with accountability. The nature of their concern has been a bit different from what has led educational institutions and professional groups to establish accountability systems. To managed health care, the motive for assigning accountability has been one of cost.

If you've been among the lucky who have not been ill in the past twenty years, you may not know that the expense of health care has escalated at a rate far exceeding the cost of living. Most Western countries have a nationalized health care system and this has partially protected them from rising costs associated with rising professional salaries. Health care in the United States is far more expensive than anywhere else in the world, yet we continue to be among the top ten countries for early infant death, and we're among the last of Western countries to offer equal benefits for mental health and physical health care under insurance programs.

Beginning in the late 1970s, the escalation of costs in the United States resulted in some modifications in the way in which health services are delivered—what we have come to know as managed health care.

Managed health care shifted the responsibility for care from a corporation-based risk or indemnity program to an assumingly more efficient, prepaid program in which the patient, the health organization, and the employers share the risk. While indemnity insurance programs still exist, they are rapidly becoming obsolete. With them has gone the flexibility of selecting among a wide range of providers, the security of unlimited coverage, and, some argue, the quality of care.

The first managed health care programs were consumed by the issue of cost. Accordingly, they severely restricted who could provide the services and who would be able to receive them. Care was largely restricted to acute care. Paradoxically, this meant that in the mental health field, expensive inpatient treatment took precedent over less expensive outpatient care since services were delayed until the problem deteriorated.

The number of outpatient visits for drug, alcohol, or mental health problems was strictly limited, usually to somewhere between eight and twenty sessions. Providers were restricted to those who successfully bid for the lowest price and met certain minimal standards of experience and training. The effectiveness of services was equated, inversely, with the cost of providing those services.

This early managed health care made patients unhappy. They had to justify the simplest services in the most extreme way and coverage for many services was frequently terminated before some of the more long-standing and difficult problems were solved. Moreover, it limited access to practitioners, and seldom allowed people to select their own doctors or providers.

In the second wave of managed health care programs, breadth of provider options increased and more options were offered with co-payments. Instead of a large organization that hired a select group of providers who in turn agreed to reduce their fees for the assurance of having steady work, capitation and "carve out" programs were adopted. Into the picture came a middleman. This person or group contracted with an employer, a state, or an insurance group to provide health and mental health services at a fixed rate per enrollee.

On the other side of the middleman, groups of providers would subcontract to deliver the services at even lower cost, for each of those who needed service. The middleman, therefore, made money by finding both cheap subcontractors and *not* delivering service. That way, they were able to keep the capitation money as profit.

Providers, on the other hand, made money if they saw large numbers of patients at reduced costs. They became dependent on those who arranged the contracts and controlled access to patients. The driving force behind this scheme was clearly some short-term cost savings. Since services are often much more expensive in the short run than doing nothing, there were incentives to provide fewer rather than better services, and even for paying the patient to avoid seeking services.

Although treatment effectiveness was still equated with how cheap the treatments were, to offset the tendency to avoid providing services, a new definition was added. Effectiveness became assessed by counting the different services provided, the number of missed appointments, and how quickly the providers returned their patient tracking forms. Effectiveness became based on cheap but accessible services, with little or no attention given to how or whether these services actually eliminated symptoms, improved lives, or reduced other medical costs.

Patient dissatisfaction with the quality of care has recently initiated a third phase in the history of managed health care in the United States. A series of legal cases, in which health management groups have been found to use unnecessary and inordinately time-consuming accounting procedures before approving treatment, has forced these groups to look once again at the actual helpfulness of the services provided, and even to reconsider the earlier decision to disallow long-term treatments. While this movement is awakening new interest in the concept of symptom improvement, it is still too early to tell whether the pull of money will be overcome as the primary definition of a treatment's efficacy and effectiveness.

The Law and the "Respectable Minority"

The courts have also been concerned with the accountability of professional mental health practice, largely because they must decide when a clinician's practice is not justified in terms of current knowledge—when it constitutes malpractice. One of the standards used is the principle of the community standard. A procedure is considered to be effective if it enjoys popular appeal. Even a more troubling principle is that of the "respectable minority." This principle is used as the basis for mediating disputes among experts to determine what treatments are valid. Thus, in short, courts have ruled that a clinician's treatments are valid and appropriate (the legal equivalent of "effectiveness") if they are either consistent with conventional practice within the community or with a "respectable minority" of practitioners who consistently follow this given theory and method.

The validity of a treatment, from this legal view, has nothing to do with how well the treatment works or the validity of the underlying theory. For example, in *Hood v. Phillips,* a malpractice action against a surgeon was not upheld, even though only six other physicians in the world used his procedure. The court accepted the respectable minority defense "despite the fact that the medical community considered the procedure (1) to be below minimum standards of medical treatment of emphysema; (2) to have no medical justification; (3) to be useless at best and potentially quite dangerous." In *Leach v. Braillar,* the court upheld a malpractice action against a physician because his procedure varied from that of the school of sixty-five physicians he claimed to follow. Had he properly adhered to the school's procedure, he could have successfully defended himself through the respectable minority rule whether the procedure worked or not.

Although no one has explicit definitions of this rule, the courts generally have considered several factors when determining the respectable minority support of a therapeutic approach. First, is there a clearly identifiable professional association that follows the approach? Second, are there specific standards of practice associated with the approach? Third, do practitioners of this approach follow articulated ethical guidelines?

The fact that an outside agency like the court could be presumed to define the nature of adequate mental health treatment, and would do so purely on the grounds of whether a given theory was accepted by a group of people, underscores the problems of not having an explicit body or group that sets standards based on scientific demonstration of effectiveness. The courts are not to blame: Judges and lawyers are not experts in science or health care, and the respectable minority rule is their way of passing responsibility on to the professions. However, it is the patient who suffers.

There is no federal Food and Drug Administration (FDA) to govern the availability of various psychotherapies. Hence, there is no set standard for defining when a given procedure has been adequately researched to see if it is a scientifically valid intervention. Therapists may believe they are practicing scientifically credible procedures when they are not, either because they are not familiar with the scientific literature or because they have a nonscientific standard of "proof" by which they judge the scientific credibility of their treatments.

The Law and the Doctrine of Informed Consent

The courts have attempted to provide other guidance in determining when a psychotherapy practice is reputable. However, they place the primary burden on the patient to get and assess information about psychotherapists. They have done this through the doctrine of informed consent.

The notion of informed consent is based on the principles of "individual autonomy, and specifically of the premise that every person has the right to determine what shall be done to his own body." Accordingly, informed consent requires that clinicians provide to the patient "sufficient information to permit the patient to make an informed and intelligent decision on whether to submit to a proposed course of treatment or surgical procedure." Informed disclosure of risk and benefits specifically includes a description of the nature of the problem, the risks of the proposed treatment, the risks of alternative treatments, and the risks of not doing anything at all.

Some believe this principle is a means of relieving clinicians from the need to evaluate their treatments or keep up with current scientific literature. Others believe that it is a viable alternative to the draconian necessity of having one's practice dictated by outsiders.

One team of theorists has provided the following list of benefits that derive from providing a clear statement to patients:

- It promotes the individual autonomy of both patient and clinician.
- It protects patients from being unknowingly exposed to experimental treatments.
- It avoids or reduces the likelihood of fraud and resultant duress.
- It encourages self-scrutiny and monitoring by groups of health professionals.
- It promotes rational decisions in treatment planning.
- It involves the treatment-seeking public in the process of developing their own treatment.

While informed consent applies quite specifically to medical treatments such as surgery, its limits have not been sufficiently defined to be very useful for less invasive treatments like those in the area of mental health. Indeed, it's questionable whether insisting on informed consent in the area of psychotherapy would be of much advantage to a prospective patient. For example, the courts continue to give much discretion to the clinician about what types of risks he or she reports to the patient. They have held that the degree of disclosure made to patients is a question of "medical judgment," and that the value of this judgment is determined by what is called the "customary standard of the profession." In other words, what is disclosed is based on its popularity in the community of clinicians rather than on factual information about effectiveness.

To judge clinical worth according to the popularity of a treatment, of course, is at best highly questionable. Moreover, there is no professional consensus that defines what should be disclosed. Invoking the doctrine of a respectable minority is a professional-based standard of proof. Again, it does not address the most important issue for the consumer of psychology—effectiveness.

Problems with this judicial standard are seen in several ways. For example, when malpractice claims are directed at a practitioner using professional standards of disclosure, the person who lodges the complaint has to provide expert witnesses to establish that neither the criteria of community standards, nor those based on the doctrine of a respectable minority, were met. You have to find professionals willing to testify against one another—a situation that encourages a conspiracy of silence among colleagues.

Because of these difficulties with the professional standard, there has been a judicial trend to modify the doctrine of disclosure and move toward one that is more patient-based. Under this rule, the standard of what should be disclosed would be based on the patient's need to know the information. The information to be provided is defined by "whether a reasonable person in the patient's position would attach significance to the information." This standard places greater importance on the informed consent doctrine as a protection of the patient's interests. It relieves plaintiffs from the need to present expert witnesses to establish the appropriate professional standard of disclosure. Instead, they must prove that the practitioner's failure to provide sufficient information prevented the patient from declining treatment. The standard is whether a "reasonable patient" would have withheld consent to the treatment or procedure had the material risks been disclosed.

On the positive side, informed consent—especially as judged by the patient-oriented procedure—ensures that a patient is an active participant in the decision-making process regarding treatment. It may also help protect you from a therapist who uses dangerous or ineffective treatments.

GUIDELINES TO KEEP IN MIND

Here are some steps to take when seeking a therapist.

Ask people you trust for therapists they have consulted. Friends and acquaintances might be better sources than physicians or members of the clergy. But physicians and clergy are certainly preferable to going through the Yellow Pages.

Once you have a list of two or more names, you should feel free to seek additional information from the therapist. Most of this information can be obtained by a phone interview, before making a commitment to enter treatment or an appointment. You should feel free to:

* Find out the person's professional training and educational history, including the professional discipline with which the therapist is identified. Make sure you know if the therapist is a physician (and what kind), a psychologist (and what kind), a counselor, a nurse, or a social worker. Also determine the highest degree the therapist has earned and where this degree was received.

* Find out the amount of experience the therapist has had in treating people with your problem.

* Find out the nature of the therapist's typical practice—the types of patients the therapist typically works with, their demographic descriptions, the length of usual treatment, what percentage become free of symptoms, and so on. Learn the therapist's success in treating people with problems like yours.

* Find out the therapist's status as a Diplomate or Fellow in a recognized professional association.

* Find out where the therapist holds staff membership—what hospitals, clinics, and health maintenance organizations.

In soliciting this information, remember that there is a pronounced but human tendency among therapists to overrate their effectiveness, level of experience, and to minimize the time needed to alleviate your problems. Also remember that people may convince you that they are generalists, effective with everyone, but this is unlikely. Most therapists are successful in treating particular problems and a narrower band of individuals—fewer than they may reveal. Ask the type of patients with whom the therapist believes he or she has had the most and least success.

Once you have obtained this information, the next step is to do a credential check. This is a two-stage process. First, obtain assurance that the therapist's credentials are real. Instead of attempting to discover information yourself about whether the clinician's alma mater is accredited, the most efficient procedure is to contact the state licensing board. You can get the telephone number from the state attorney general's office. This will not assure you that the therapist is any good, but it will eliminate most fraudulent individuals.

The second step is to check on the professional groups in which the clinician holds credentials as a Fellow or Diplomate. Again, the state licensing board that oversees the profession with which the therapist identifies should be able to provide information about whether these groups are legitimate and credible (see Appendix).

As you proceed, also remember that the meaning of the term "effectiveness" differs as a function of who is defining it. It's helpful to ask what the therapist means by this term, and to inquire about how he or she reconciles the different viewpoints of "effectiveness" provided by managed care and the usual clinical reliance on symptom improvement. Solicit some examples of treatment that will give you an idea of what to expect. Ask your therapist to give you information and references that document the scientific validity and effectiveness of the treatments to be used.

Of course, none of these procedures will ensure that the therapist you select is good, effective, or helpful. However, they will help identify poorly trained therapists, ones who are misrepresenting themselves, and those who use ineffective treatments. They also do little to address the problem of finding a therapist whose personal characteristics are therapeutic. Complete protection from therapists whose personalities are noxious or whose skill is deficient is not possible, anymore than it is possible to ensure against this problem in medical practice. And yet we seem more vigilant with medical doctors and our medical problems then we are with mental health workers.

In the next chapter, we try to offer additional ways of determining which therapists will be a good match for particular problems.

4

—————— ~ ——————

Seeking the Healing
Patient–Therapist
Relationship

Patty P had just finished her master's degree in chemistry from a prestigious New England university and had been accepted into a science journalism program in the Midwest. She was already beginning to pack, physically and mentally.

Patty's fiancé, Howie, was attending a medical school in the South and Patty had dated other men while they were separated. She was ambivalent about Howie and her future with him, wondering why, after she had agreed to marry him, she was still attracted to—and even slept with—other men. With a new stage in her life beginning, and with too much self-doubt, she decided to seek help.

She found an ad for a psychologist in her school newspaper—Dr. M, who specialized in relationship problems and cognitive therapy. Her first appointment with Dr. M was successful. He was in his mid-thirties, urbane, and she liked his "scientific" approach to therapy—his emphasis on how to communicate better.

Usually, Patty was Dr. M's last appointment of the day. After a few sessions, they fell into a common pattern. Following her one-hour session, they went on to discuss his problems. He told her that he had just moved to the city from California and had left a girlfriend behind. He had feelings similar to her own about his relationship, wondering whether he wanted to enter into the commitment of marriage. Patty found herself acting as Dr. M's advisor.

At first, Patty was flattered that Dr. M was paying so much attention to her insights and advice, and, she admitted, enjoyed the attention. He would call her at home after a session to ask if she was all right. He said she had seemed troubled when she left the office and just wanted to check on her. She soon began calling him during the week when she was troubled or having doubts about herself.

One day Dr. M recommended a "progressive relaxation" exercise, a verbal back rub, as he described it. She was a bit startled by the suggestion. There was a subtle but unavoidable sexual undercurrent to the conversation.

After the next session, Dr. M bragged about what a great lover he was. Apparently, any woman who slept with him became permanently sexually aroused, he claimed. There was a clear hint in his tone. Patty found herself attracted and interested in the prospects of a "closer" relationship, even thinking that if she and Dr. M were to have a sexual relationship, it would make it easier to talk to him: he would know her so much better then. She asked him if having a sexual relationship wasn't unethical, but he didn't seem to think so and told her how special she was.

"I've never done anything like that with a patient," he said.

Patty, who admitted being a natural flirt, began to toy with her therapist and he responded in kind. She began to consider having an affair more seriously. It was not long before Dr. M suggested that they meet a bit later one night and maybe have some dinner afterward. Within two weeks, Patty and Dr. M made love for the first time and soon it became a regular practice after their sessions.

One afternoon, Patty met a friend, Terry, whom she had referred to Dr. M during the winter. Terry was visibly upset. Dr. M had made a pass at her, using some of the same lines Patty had heard. Patty, furious, stormed into her next session, screaming, threatening to file a complaint with the state licensing board, and then marched out. Dr. M called her daily for the next few weeks, apologizing profusely, emphasizing that Terry had misunderstood his attentions, and asking forgiveness. Once he said that he was getting psychotherapy himself. This didn't absolve Patty's feelings. She quit seeing him.

"What this experience did was alienate me from the entire psychotherapeutic community," she now says. "Those therapists, they were nothing but . . . but . . . humans!!"

Patty and Howie eventually married and she went back into therapy. She feels better now. Still bitter, but better.

This chapter is about the therapeutic relationship. We will talk about both its positive and negative attributes. A therapeutic relationship is precious; it is the primary force of healing. As in the above story, however, sometimes the careful balance between caring and exploiting is violated. In this chapter we will discuss these boundary violations and how to recognize them, and we will look at the healing qualities of a therapeutic relationship. Throughout, we will be moving back and forth between descriptions of things to avoid and those to cherish. While a little confusing, this juxtaposition is necessary because almost every positive attribute can be misused and turned into a negative one in the course of psychotherapy. We believe that you will be best served by knowing both the bad and the good, and how to recognize the difference.

Boundary Violations

Was Dr. M unethical and destructive, or helpful and caring? It could be he was all these. Clearly, his behavior was both unethical and illegal. It follows a common pattern. Violations of professional boundaries, like making sexual advances, are usually preceded by certain cues, few of which are problematic in themselves, but together they serve as signals that the therapist's professional and personal roles are merging. Phone calls are initiated; they become more frequent and longer; sessions become longer and may be changed to occur at the end of the day; fees may be reduced or delayed payment may be approved; the therapist may ask for favors such as babysitting services; the therapist may offer gifts; and sometimes, the fee may be bartered to allow the patient to work with the therapist.

Not all patients who go through such merged or violated relationships find it harmful, incidentally. Some even report that it was helpful and beneficial to them. So, we meet a conundrum. Can something be wrong and still be helpful? The answer is "Yes" because the definition of what is wrong, in this instance, is a legal and ethical decision, independent of the effects or the beliefs of either patient or therapist.

In 1968, the first breach-of-trust case pertaining to psychotherapy came to court. A Mrs. Zipkin complained that a Dr. Freeman, her psychiatrist, had enticed her to have sex with him, giving her a special place in his life and practice, and then had withdrawn it after a considerable amount of time. The two had traveled together and Mrs. Zipkin even lived and worked on Dr. Freeman's farm to pay for her therapy. The court ruled that the acts of Dr. Freeman would have been illegal, even if they had not involved sex and even if they were helpful to Mrs. Zipkin. According to the court decision, allowing the professional relationship to become personal constituted a breach of Mrs. Zipkin's trust, independent of its effects and form.

It does not matter to the rule of law that Dr. M may have helped Patty, or even that a sexual relationship itself may, under some circumstances, improve a patient's mood and feeling of well-being. It is a violation of law and of the professional practitioner's ethics.

Sexual indiscretions are the behaviors most likely reported in the local newspaper and the ones that result in the most serious reprimands and sanctions from legal bodies and licensing boards.

However, these also are acts that, no matter how serious, occur less frequently than either the failure to help or the production of harm through ignorance.

Approximately 3 percent of female therapists and as many as 10 percent of male therapists admit that they have been guilty of illicit sexual acts with patients. Women are most often the ones affected and surveys suggest that about 5 percent of women ex-patients report having been harassed or sexually involved with their therapists. Seventy percent of these indicate that the experience was harmful. This seems like a large percentage—too large. It justifies the sanctions that are placed against therapist boundary violations—violations of trust. But we don't know what constitutes harm, in this case, and it is unclear why 30 percent of female patients report that the experience either did not do harm or actually was beneficial. How could one feel helped by such illegal and unethical behavior? Perhaps because it conveyed love and caring, for all the potential damaging messages that it may also carry.

From a scientific perspective we also need to know more about the nature of these acts and their consequences. Obtaining a scientific answer to these questions would depend on having a representative sample of individuals who participated in such activities with their therapists. Scientifically, there are no ways at present to ensure that the patient would have improved more had the therapist not violated a professional boundary.

From a legal perspective, you should understand that it doesn't matter if such acts on the part of the therapist are harmful or not. They are illegal in many states and unethical in all. As the court said in the case of Dr. Freeman, the issue is that a boundary has been violated and a trust betrayed, not what the consequence of that act is.

What Characteristics Make a Therapist Effective?

Research provides assurance that a therapist who is able to provide a safe and caring atmosphere is likely to be therapeutic. Research also gives us some information on the specific acts and practices that make this relationship seem warm and caring, but it is more silent on what acts, practices, and therapist characteristics inhibit and impede the progress of psychotherapy. We must understand both what facilitates and what inhibits progress. For the moment, we are concerned about the characteristics that therapists bring into a relationship, not those behaviors and procedures that occupy their time once they begin treatment.

While good results depend on the therapist's ability to convey emphatic concern, trustworthiness, and expertise, the patient also plays a major role. A motivated patient, one who is persistent, cooperative, and introspective, is likely to do better than one who lacks these qualities. Lack of progress can also arise from the failure of either participant or therapist to maintain the honesty and motivation that are needed to ensure growth.

Conveying understanding requires that the therapist be a partner with the patient. For most patients, this sense of partnership is enhanced if the therapist's conversation, activity, and direction are consistent with the patient's expectations. Your therapist should not interrupt you, should keep appointments, and should be respectful of your experiences. Sometimes, a therapist's theoretical beliefs prevent him from providing suggestions to you, and he may feel he shouldn't offer direct advice or make judgments about your behavior. This is often the case with therapists who adopt a psychoanalytic approach to therapy. Other therapists are active, however, and many readily provide guidance or suggestions, even helping you to practice things that are discussed. One patient may enjoy this level of activity, while another will find that it feels disruptive and disrespectful. If a therapist does not respond with the level of guidance and activity that you would like, you should talk to her about this. Remember, the therapist works for you and it is her responsibility to provide a response from which you can benefit. It is not unreasonable to expect the therapist to tell you what kind of response you can expect from her, and to try adapting to your requests.

Most patients, new to therapy, do not like or want a therapist who is passive. They want their therapist to do more than just sit there and listen without response. These patients want a therapist who will give them feedback, will ask questions, and even give advice. If the therapist either fails to explain these roles or does not offer the style of relationship in which you feel supported and understood, this therapist may not be the one to help you. Even if therapists, because of their theoretical predilections, are inclined to be quite silent, you certainly have the right to expect and request a more active approach if you prefer one.

By saying that it is important for a patient to feel cared for and understood, we do not mean to imply that you will have this feeling all the time. The relationship must also learn to tolerate anger. Both therapists and patients get angry and both must learn to work through these feelings and find some resolution. Some research suggests that progress is better when the relationship is sometimes challenged and then healed. Getting angry at your therapist is normal, but the failure to resolve this anger within a session or two probably bodes poorly for continued progress.

Another aspect of the therapist's behavior that contributes to your sense of being understood is the therapist's willingness to talk about the therapy relationship itself. An effective therapist will at least occasionally raise the question of how you feel about the therapy and will encourage you to talk about it, both the good and the not-so-good aspects.

There are at least three things that a therapist could do that can make you worse. One is to be critical and caustic. Critical humor directed at the patient doesn't help. This usually results from the therapist's failure to control his or her own defensive anger.

Yes, it is possible for you to make even the best therapist angry or hurt. We are human. But a therapist's failure to deal well with anger is probably the most frequent cause of a patient getting worse. If a therapist becomes overtly angry, insists that his view is more correct than yours, and seems to compete with you for who's the most important or knowledgeable, you have a problem. A therapist must be sufficiently nondefensive that he can allow you to win, to be right, and to be safe from fear of criticism.

A hostile therapist, one who is critical, disrespectful, and insensitive is not helpful. If the moment of anger passes and resolves without your feeling put down, the relationship may be salvageable. If it does not pass within a few sessions, or if it is frequent, you might consider discussing it and then seek help elsewhere.

A therapist who is critical and judgmental is also ineffective, and can even be damaging. A therapist who seems to see, as a major part of the job, the task of pointing out your faults will probably be ineffective and may actually prevent growth. Good and effective therapists try to help you see your strengths—frequently, aspects of yourself that you have failed to appreciate. They spend at least as much time observing and commenting on your strengths as on your failures.

Another countertherapeutic behavior of a therapist comes from the mismatch of style and technique with your needs. Sometimes, therapists provide directives and suggestions. These suggestions can be helpful if they are wanted and followed. However, if you find them disruptive, and if you're not acting on them, it may be that the therapist's approach is the problem. Before you question your own worth and value for not following the directions, raise the question with your therapist whether this is a productive approach. If your uneasiness continues, it may be a sign that the two of you are incompatible.

There may be exceptions to this guideline.

One of the authors [BB] knows a middle-aged women who underwent extensive therapy for depression. She had gained 100 pounds and she and her husband spent most of their time arguing. He was upset that she had let herself fall into such an emotional and physical hole. She went to a classically trained psychoanalyst, who sat silently taking notes while she talked. She blossomed. For the first time in her life someone took her seriously and listened to what she said. She went four times a week (she had wealthy parents) and was never happier. She lost weight, looked better, and she and her husband put an end to their bickering.

After four years, she faced an important decision: whether to move back to the town where she grew up. Her parents had offered to set her and her husband up in business. Unable to make up her mind, she asked her therapist for advice. After four years of almost complete silence he finally spoke:

"I think it's a wonderful opportunity. You should go back," he said.

It was the worst decision she ever made. She spent the next half dozen years in misery.

You can draw your own conclusions from this true story, but it is important to remember that patients are responsible for their own decisions, despite the best recommendations of therapists. This case is particularly ironic because psychoanalysts rarely find it advantageous to converse freely with their patients.

The Therapeutic Relationship

A therapist who is able to make the patient feel supported and understood is likely to be effective. How does a therapist do that? Why is it so hard to describe an effective therapist? Partly, it is the nature of the person with whom she is working—the patient. A therapist may be very effective for one person and not very helpful with another. For one patient, a laid-back and quiet therapist conveys support.

Another patient views this behavior as a sign of disinterest. Without knowing who the patient is, we can only define an effective therapist in general terms.

Generally, an effective therapist is one who cares, is attentive, makes few critical judgments, doesn't interfere, and offers a level of activity that is consistent with the patient's particular expectations and preferences. It is hard to imagine that any therapist, no matter what she does, can be very effective without being attentive, caring, and nonjudgmental. Assuming these caring qualities, a few other attributes characterize the maximally effective therapist.

Differences That Make a Difference

Common sense, let alone scientific research, should convince us that while a kind and caring therapist is a good thing, each patient should also be treated differently. Some patients will benefit from one therapist some from another. The myth of uniformity—that all therapists and approaches to psychotherapy are about equal and alike—is unfortunately pervasive and implicitly shared by significant elements within the health care system despite its illogic.

Managed health care, for instance, has consistently made the inaccurate assumption that all patients with a given diagnosis are similar and warrant the same type of therapist and the same treatment. Indeed, diagnosis is the major patient factor used in determining length of care, nature of care, and location or setting of care. Yet, *diagnosis is among the least important characteristics that set one patient apart from another when trying to tailor treatment to individual needs.* We explore this observation in greater details in the next chapter. Belief in the importance of patient labeling for treatment assignment is but one of several myths that have prevented patients from getting the treatment that they need and deserve.

Another of these myths, and one we will give greater attention to here, is the belief that all psychotherapy is equal. Acceptance of this myth on the part of managed health care systems has resulted in decisions to limit all outpatient treatment to eight or twelve or twenty sessions, or to provide the cheapest psychotherapy by those who charge the lowest fees. A more logical and appealing response would be to discard these myths and assign the length of treatment, the therapist's training level, and the nature of the treatment to the patient as variables in deciding what sorts of treatment are likely to work for particular individuals.

Consider two patients with the same symptoms of depression. One is male and one is female. One copes with depression by getting angry and getting drunk; the other withdraws and avoids people. One resents anyone who tries to help, and the other seeks all the assistance she can find. Because they show the same diagnostic symptoms—unhappiness, loss of appetite, low self-esteem, loss of sexual and social interest—they may get the same therapist, be allowed the same twelve sessions of treatment, and be put on the same medication. But what if patterns of coping, rebellion, and withdrawal among other things, have more to do with what treatments will be effective than the diagnosis and symptoms?

We have considerable research evidence that the patient who deals with depression by acting out and getting drunk requires a very different and a longer treatment than the patient who becomes withdrawn. The rebellious one will respond worse to a therapist who is active and directive and will probably not be helped by medication compared with the compliant patient. One patient may require a highly experienced and trained therapist, while another does not. Systems that assign all patients to the same therapists, the same lengths of treatment, and the same demands ignore the differences we see in our patients.

What Characteristics of the Therapist Encourage Success?

Although research has failed to find convincing evidence that therapist experience has a significant and consistent effect on treatment outcome, this research is sufficiently flawed and the stakes sufficiently high that we include these characteristics among those that should be considered when selecting a therapist. We believe some patients, particularly those with long-standing and complex problems, should be assigned highly trained and experienced therapists while this is less important for others.

Experience and Skill

Therapists' advertisements frequently refer to their experience, and many practicing therapists assume that experience and training are always important, if not necessary, for effective treatment. Managed health care organizations, however, frequently assume just the opposite—that there is little relationship between being an effective therapist and one's level of training or experience, at least beyond some minimal training. Recognizing the paucity of research evidence, many academic researchers have also concluded that experience and training are irrelevant.

We interpret the research somewhat differently, although we acknowledge that most of those who seek or receive help for emotional problems will benefit from therapists who are good and caring people, regardless of their level or type of training. There are, however, dangers in deciding to assign a therapist with little professional training to a new patient seeking help.

Just as therapists may overstate the magnitude of the relationship between skill and experience, contemporary research may understate it. By accepting the passage of time as the definition of "experience," researchers have assumed that all activities occurring since graduation are equivalent.

Logically, the passage of time alone does not constitute an adequate research definition either of training or experience. Formal training varies considerably from program to program and discipline to discipline, with few consistent or common standards. As a result, fledgling mental health professionals differ widely in clinical experience and skill when they enter practice.

And a therapist can spend considerable time since graduation in ways that don't make him or her a better therapist. You would never survey radiologists whose practices don't include surgery, to see if time since their graduation makes them better surgeons. Why should we compare non-therapists who have spent their professional careers consulting with business managers on effective employment practices, those who have spent each day seeing a complex array of difficult and demanding patients, and those who have changed career tracks and become lawyers and plumbers?

Perhaps equally misleading is that this research equates the amount of effort and time it takes to adequately learn all available therapy procedures. Some procedures may require fifteen years to learn well. Why compare them to those you can learn in three weeks? If surgeons who practice only tonsillectomies—a relatively simple skill learned early in medical training—are included along with surgeons who practice only complex brain surgery, skills that require years to perfect, the result is likely to underrate the role of experience on skill.

An even more likely possibility might explain the research findings. Most of the skills used by therapists on a majority of patients require little specific practice; yet highly complex and difficult skills are needed to successfully treat a minority of patients. The results consequently would underestimate the effects of experience.

What is clear is that the effectiveness of specific procedures cannot logically be assessed without knowing the nature of the patients and their problems. Moreover, it is intuitively logical that there is an inherent danger in using minimally trained therapists without consideration of the severity and responsiveness of the patient's problems.

We are not suggesting that only highly trained and experienced therapists should serve as mental health providers. Rational treatment assignments must discriminate cases that may be more difficult from others. By far most people who seek treatment will improve, as long as the therapist is consistent, considerate, and available during the time it takes patients to sort through their problems and work out solutions.

If your problems have developed recently, do not affect your ability to work and take care of yourself, and appear to be reacting to changes and demands in your life, they are likely to respond positively to a therapist who allows you to think through your difficulties, and who encourages patience. Indeed, most people who seek help (we think it is probably between 70 and 80 percent, though some experts believe this percentage is much lower) will get help from their psychotherapist, even if they have very complex and difficult problems.

This occurs to the degree that the therapist can provide care, understanding, and warm support.

These skills of listening, caring, and instilling hope are not all that is involved in psychotherapy, however. Especially if your problems are more long-standing, difficult, recurrent, and do not seem directly related to situational stresses, you may need skilled therapists who can tailor treatment to your specific problems. If you are one of these patients, we believe that you should seek out a therapist with doctoral-level-training (M.D.s or Ph.D.s) because they are more likely to have had the specialized instruction you may need.

Not getting this kind of specialized help when you need it may make problems worse. That is, they may have an accumulating effect and come to interfere more and more with your efforts to become happy and successful. For example, hypnosis is a specialized technique that is very effective as a means of controlling anxiety or physical pain. But hypnosis may be of no more benefit than a period of relaxation or rest for those who have a transitory problem of limited severity. Indeed, it may contribute to damage for those who are pursuing forgotten—and fictitious—memories of abuse.

Flexibility and Creativity

A creative and flexible mind is even less easily defined than experience. A good therapist has such a mind. He or she can perceive new ways of approaching problems, come up with novel ideas for viewing your problem, and suggest new ways of learning adaptive skills. These techniques and insights go beyond skill and reveal the "art" of psychotherapy.

Art and science are not enemies. The painter operates within the bounds of physical laws—blue and yellow make green; when two objects occur in close juxtaposition, they appear related, and so on. The effective artist works within these rules to apply novel contexts and interpretations. In the same way, the effective therapist is more than a technician who applies sterile technologies to solve problems. Talented therapists use the principles of effective intervention to construct new and novel ways of helping people learn.

For example, one of us (LB) trains horses in his spare time. In the process of watching expert and inexpert trainers, you can begin to see the difference between those who are merely technicians and those who are experts—it is creativity. And it is a key factor in being a good therapist as well.

Both novice and expert trainers can learn to operate from the same behavioral principles. They can understand the importance and use of reward and punishment, the necessity of immediate consequences, and the value of establishing a sensitivity for the motives and reasoning processes of the horse. By knowing how to use these principles, even a novice horse trainer can learn to teach a horse complex skills, such as running in circles and figure-eights, and coming when signaled—at least when both horse and trainer toil in closely confined and controlled space. But getting beyond that safety zone and translating the principles to large, uncontrolled areas requires more than knowledge; it requires creativity.

The creative resources of the novice therapist are exhausted quickly, and few without experience have the creative resources to create the novel environments that will work for the complex patient. Experience and flexibility are necessary to either create new environments in which the principles may operate or apply those principles to never-before-attempted tasks.

Similarly, most of us with some effort can learn to perform the technical procedures of various psychotherapies. These skills are not often very complex. They involve methods for conveying interest, ways of understanding unspoken meanings and translating these for the patient, and the performance of certain stock procedures for directing the patient's practice of newly learned behaviors through homework or in the therapy session.

For many problems and people, therapists with minimal formal training and technical proficiency may be fine. But if the problem presented is novel, complex, or unresponsive to stock methods, it takes a flexible and creative therapist to facilitate change. Education and years of experience are no guarantee that a therapist will have a creative solution to your problems, but these factors increase the probability that the therapist has the ability to help.

Of course, beyond these qualities, the therapist must also have technical expertise. Later in the book, we turn to the specialized skills and knowledge that are necessary for the therapist to acquire.

GUIDELINES TO KEEP IN MIND

Central to determining if a given therapist is good for you is a question only you can answer: "Am I comfortable with this therapist? Do we connect?"

A therapist who is disrespectful, critical, caustic, and angry will unlikely achieve a warm and safe atmosphere in which you can explore your concerns and fears effectively. Disrespect is signaled by the therapist being late for appointments, tolerating interruptions during the session, and forgetting important information about you and your problem. You have a right to expect that the therapist will remember things that are important to you, will give you the courtesy of keeping appointments, informing you in advance when she is unable to do so, and will attend to you rather than burdening you with her problems and past history. Beyond this general recommendation, we suggest the following considerations in deciding if a therapist is suited to you.

* The therapy relationship must be able to tolerate anger, but anger should be a minor part of the emotions that are present between patient and therapist.
* Anger might appear, but it should never control the relationship.
* The therapist should be kind and open, have a willingness to talk about the problems in the therapy relationship, and respect your goals and concerns.

In the midst of problems and anxieties, people often forget that they still have strengths, assets, and skills. One often-forgotten characteristic of an effective therapist is that they help remind you that you have strengths and unique qualities.

Besides anger, there are other characteristics to look out for that may indicate an ineffective and destructive therapist. The following indicators should signal to you that there are problems. You should terminate treatment with a therapist:

* If the therapist cannot keep professional and personal roles separate. A departure from professional ethics could mean a failure in self-control, self-respect, and respect for you.
* If the therapist makes sexual advances to you, even if both of you think that it would neither be harmful nor unhelpful. This is unethical behavior and is not tolerated by any standards of behavior set by the profession.
* If the therapist discloses information about your treatment, even to acknowledge that you are in treatment, without your explicit consent. This kind of behavior breaches the confidentiality that you should be able to expect from practicing professionals. It is a serious violation of the ethical codes of behavior.

Finally, experienced and highly trained therapists (usually Ph.D.s or M.D.s) may be needed for very complex, long-standing, and recurrent problems you may be having. Typically, these require time and patience. In contrast, highly trained therapists may not be necessary for many problems, especially those occurring as single episodes that are reactions to events in your life.

Think about what troubles you. Is it the result of a new person in your life, a new job, a new boss? Has this problem been waking you up at night, keeping you from attending parties, from working, from facing the morning?

Even if you follow all those steps, getting the right therapist for your particular problem may still be a matter of trial and error. There is no substitute for trying a few sessions to see if you and the therapist are compatible.

Keep in mind that the effectiveness of the therapist is not related to how fast the treatment works. It takes some time, often two or three months, before you will notice much change in your life and help in solving your problems. If you find yourself liking and trusting the therapist, this bodes well for continuing the relationship.

5

How Helpful Is Diagnosis?

A *New Yorker* cartoon shows a cocktail party obviously in a posh, upper-class apartment. Each guest is wearing a sign—"schizophrenic," "manic-depressive," "depressed," "paranoid"—you get the picture. Harold, who is attaching the signs, is confronted by a woman who demands, "Harold, why must you always label everyone?"

Sometimes, jumping to a diagnosis in the field of mental health can have tragic results. In 1935, the great American composer George Gershwin went to seek help for severe headaches. He ended up at the office of a psychoanalyst, who assumed he had a "neurotic" disorder and put Gershwin into deep therapy. The therapy lasted for two years. On July 11, 1937, Gershwin died of a brain tumor.

No one knows if Gershwin would have lived had someone reached the correct diagnosis—even today malignant brain tumors are untreatable—but surely he would have been spared considerable guilt, anxiety, discomfort, and the psychological pain had the tumor been diagnosed. Think of the precious time he wasted being treated for the wrong thing.

Diagnosis also has more direct social consequences. It permits some people to get paid. Therapists and physicians get paid for treating those who are ill. It removes guilt and it overemphasizes the pathology in normal behavior. Not all of these things are bad, but to decide what ones might be, we should inspect the processes that have led up to and maintain diagnosis in mental health treatment.

What Is Diagnosis in Mental Health?

Diagnosis is the process of applying labels to describe people's problems. Medical doctors do it—you have appendicitis, ulcers, heart disease, or cancer. Dentists do it—you have periodontal disease, cavities, an abscessed tooth. Psychotherapists do it too—you are paranoid, bipolar or manic-depressive, depressed, schizophrenic.

Did you notice a difference in the phrasing?

In medicine, people *have* conditions. In mental health, people *are* their conditions. They are depressed, schizophrenic, bipolar, anxious. This is not a simple matter of differences in terminology. It represents how our society—and particularly how mental health practitioners—thinks of people with emotional and behavioral problems. It is part of the social construction of mental diseases. By way of these differences in phrasing, people may lose their individual identities, at least partially, when labels are applied so decisively to them.

To understand this point, remember that one difference between medical diagnoses and those in mental health is that the latter are largely social constructs, rather than diseases of the body. Albeit that some conditions are heavily influenced by biological factors, for example, schizophrenia and manic-depressive illness, all diagnostic categories in the field of mental health rely on social behavior—they are in effect reflections of social judgments that are placed on behaviors that we find discomforting and disturbing.

Mental health diagnoses are not accurate and direct reflections of physical conditions, even when they include physical conditions. If you have a virus, you have an alien creature inside your body doing vile things. Not so in mental health. What is more important, identifying what is and is not included as a mental "disorder" serves certain social and political ends.

Social values determine what behavior is acceptable and what behavior is not, and unacceptable behavior can be called a disorder. The types of behaviors identified as "disordered" change as the values of society change. In medicine, an ulcer is an ulcer, even though the means of diagnosing and treating it may change. In mental health, different disorders come and go, the frequency of their being assigned waxes and wanes, and even the symptoms change from time to time, all by cultural, sociological, and political processes. A few decades ago, psychiatrists classified homosexuality as a mental disorder; however, pressure from gay and lesbian political coalitions forced the American Psychiatric Association (APA) to reassess its approach to homosexuality, and now it has been largely removed from the official list of disorders and diseases. Whether a behavior is a mental disorder or just a variation of normal behavior arises from these kinds of social valuing processes.

These values, at least as much as any gains we may make in our knowledge about behaviors, determine how we will think about emotional disorders, what symptoms will be defined as "illnesses," and who gets the responsibility for correcting the problems defined.

The Social Construction of Mental Illnesses

The U.S. Bureau of the Census first classified disordered behavior. In 1840, census workers identified individuals with disturbing behavior and classified them as either "idiots" (that was the scientific term at the time, implying that these individuals lacked intellectual abilities) or "insane," implying that they engaged in socially unacceptable and unusual behavior.

From the outset, these diagnoses served clear political and social purposes: to maintain records, to track problems in society, to allow or prevent the use of certain resources. Few people then believed in the concept of mental or emotional illness, and doctors assigned little value to these labels for medical purposes. At some point, diagnoses became reified—they became treated as if they were true or real entities instead of abstract constructs—in the minds of clinicians and the public. In 1952, the American Psychiatric Association published the first systematic and uniform list of "diseases of the mind" and their associated behaviors, called the *Diagnostic and Statistical Manual,* DSM for short.

From the beginning, both the identity of the illnesses included in the official DSM and their symptoms were defined by vote. That might strike you as a very democratic way of defining illnesses, except that only those who made the diagnoses, treated the conditions, and otherwise financially benefited by having a large number of individuals qualifying for their services did the voting. There was little effort to ensure, through the solicitation of independent evidence, that these behaviors arose from true diseases. A strong belief by the membership was sufficient for distinguishing between what was a problem of morality and what was a problem of illness. As a result, the nature of mental illness has always reflected the changes in moral temperament and values of the time.

When, in 1979, the third edition of the *Diagnostic and Statistical Manual* (DSM-III) removed homosexuality as a "disease," the behaviors had not changed, only the social acceptance, significance, and value given to them by society and political forces.

Between the mid-1960s and the 1990s, societal acceptance grew for explaining behaviors as a product of their psychological roots. Over this period, an increasingly large variety of behaviors, previously attributed to lack of self-control or lack of morals, became identified as "psychological illnesses." As the view that social ills were at the root of these "illnesses of the mind" grew, the legal sanctions and prerogatives of diagnosing and treating these illnesses were extended beyond the medically trained to those who held degrees in social work, sociology, religion, and psychology. Expanding the workforce was probably necessary since the number of behaviors being identified as "illnesses" was exploding. The number of professionals expanded as the number of disorders that needed treating grew—probably not a coincidence.

Of course, the fact that insurance carriers promised to pay for the treatment of those who met the criteria of mental illness established by the American Psychiatric Association may have had something to do with the process of including more and more behaviors under the umbrella of "illness."

Between 1952 and 1968, the number of accepted "diseases of the mind" grew from 66 to 111, but by 1994, when the most recent DSM-IV was published, the number of disorders recognized by the association was up to 397. Through forty years and four editions, the number of disorders had increased exponentially as finer distinctions were made among symptoms, and as more mental health practitioners came to identify certain classes and groups of behaviors as being in need of correction.

In the short time between the publication of the DSM-IIIR in 1987 and DSM-IV in 1994, either the labels or the criteria used to identify over 120 disorders were changed; thirteen disorders were added; and eight other conditions were eliminated. Such one-time popular concepts, like "neurosis," a term we have all heard, was deleted and later reinvented with a different set of accompanying symptoms. Other categories were first introduced and then voted out of existence because it was felt that they were sexist. While it may be possible that these changes really reflect a solid change in the scientific bases of knowledge, it appears more likely that they indicate efforts to adapt to a society whose values change. We doubt that cancer or heart disease could be voted in and out of existence because they were sexist or unfavorable or lacking in political sensitivity. If they were voted out of existence, would they cease to exist and to kill people? We think that such evidence clearly demonstrates that mental health diagnoses are subject to sometimes powerful political influences and are, therefore, also subject to abuse by those forces.

A society that would rather identify disharmonious behaviors as illnesses, addictions, and disorders than problems of morality, discipline, self-knowledge, or criminality may have had something to do with the process. Perhaps the medicalization of deviant behavior is endemic to a political system that has exhausted the usual methods of control and seeks desperately to find some way of controlling unacceptable and disturbing behaviors. Treating "sick" or "addicted" individuals is preferable to acknowledging that deviant individuals may voluntarily choose socially destructive and immoral behavior. That would require that we accept the failures and weaknesses of an open, democratic society.

Applying the democratic process to the election and cure of disease seems to be a reasonable and politically sustaining tactic. When one of the top forensic experts on multiple personality, Margaret Singer of the University of California at Berkeley, was asked to comment on the specifics and origins of another colleague's diagnosis of Ken Bianchi, the Hillside Strangler, Singer startled the PBS interviewer. She said we don't really know what creates such monsters—he may simply be evil.

How much more acceptable it is to call someone like this ill, or to say he is schizophrenic or paranoid. We contend that the more scientifically sounding terms applied to diagnosis offer little or no more information than the philosophical term "evil." We maintain that the diagnostic terms, however, partly protect society from a sense of helplessness that terms like evil convey. Were such behaviors less medical, we'd have to confront the nature of a family and society that fosters such behavior and, maybe, even deal with the serious questions of the existence and teleology of evil. With medical terms, even though they explain little, we then have a reason to implement strong institutional controls such as the use of drugs and hospitalization.

The Medicalization of Deviant Behavior

Our discussion of DSM shows us clearly that the categories of deviant behavior voted on from time to time reflect social and political conventions. Depending on the disorder, the sociopolitical role played by diagnoses is either great or small, but the application of a diagnosis is always, to a greater or lesser degree, embracing political and social values.

Diagnostic labels define what limits of difference society can tolerate. Whenever a culture decides that it will define a set of behaviors as "sick" rather than "immoral" or unwitting, it is enacting a social value that favors illness over the view that such destructive or unusual behavior is volitional. Armed with this view of behavior as illness, we can justify forced hospitalization, prison, or "protective care."

Consider, however, that unlike medical diagnoses, most mental and behavioral diagnoses cannot be defined separately from their behaviors. Regardless of whatever may be happening in one's chemistry or physiology, *if behavior is not disordered, there is no condi-*

tion. With few exceptions, the diagnosis is only a restatement of the symptoms, not a determination of their cause. Unlike physical medicine where a diagnosis such as hypertension can still be asymptomatic, there is no mental health condition that can exist without symptoms. You can't be depressed or have a major depression without some of the following behavioral symptoms:

- Loss of social interest such as decreasing social activities
- Sadness
- Change of appetite
- Change in sexual interest
- Altered sleep patterns
- Slowing of mental processes
- Feelings of worthlessness and helplessness

The same holds true for all other mental health or psychiatric diagnoses. They cannot and do not exist apart from their manifestations in a person's complaints or behaviors.

In medicine, the condition is not dependent on the symptom. The symptom only assists in making the diagnosis; it doesn't determine it. You may have no gastric distress or other manifest symptoms, but still have an ulcer. Many people, unfortunately, have cancer long before they have symptoms. But we define mental illnesses by subjective reports and overt behaviors. By definition, the symptoms must be present.

The identification of psychiatric disorders always involves a social judgment and often implies a political agenda as well. The definition that behavior constitutes a "problem" for clinical purposes hinges both on what society desires—a social judgment—and what is disruptive of the political order and values—the political agenda. It is less concerned with what is true than with what values it supports and maintains. Research, though also influenced by political forces, is less driven by them than are clinical judgments. Because research methods are less culture specific and are, by their nature, open to replication, the findings may be more likely to be reasonably objective and free from politics. But research needs funding, and political forces and our culture influence such funding decisions.

For example, the Reagan administration eliminated designated research on social problems and psychosocial treatments. This decision did not eliminate such research, but it did reduce it. Scientists either redirected their programs toward biological treatments or reconstructed and recast their research programs as being focused on the "brain," a concept that was at once sufficiently nebulous and legitimate, as well as sufficiently abstract. While political forces could alter the priority and prevalence of particular research, they could not change the results of specific programs.

There are other examples of how political forces alter the nature of diagnosis and treatment. For example, as we pointed out earlier, people diagnosed as depressed frequently are more accurate in assessing the likelihood of unwanted consequences of their behavior than those who are "normal." Nondepressed individuals distort the facts through rose-colored glasses to stay "happy." If a good grasp of reality was a concept that truly was desired by society, why would we not consider depressed persons as uniquely gifted? For two reasons: Happiness is more highly valued by our society than realism—the social judgment in this diagnosis. And happiness is more likely to maintain the current political balance than unhappiness. Political power is maintained by keeping the most people happy. If they fail at this, eventually, the system will give way to a more promising alternative. Witness the USSR. As long as communism was the only viable alternative, it persisted. When an alternative became apparent and the political door opened wide enough to allow this alternative to be seen as a possibility, communism collapsed under the pressure of those who were unhappy.

Language and Treatment

Notice that even as *we* write about it, we often identify people as being depressed, unhappy, and so on, rather than as having the condition. It is hard to do otherwise, revealing the degree to which such conceptions are entrenched in our society. In the face of this tendency, it is sometimes difficult to remember that there is a real difference between having a certain condition and being a certain condition. The idea of having a condition implies that it is only one aspect of your being—it does not own you; it is often temporary, correctable, and treatable. To be depressed, schizophrenic, or whatever, implies that it is an indelible part of your identity, a characteristic that you carry with you, and that successful treatment will require that you give up.

While mental health practitioners are taught not to equate the condition with the person, the fact that it usually shows up in the language of the field signals something about what we have come to believe about mental, emotional, and behavioral problems.

Our language determines and reflects how we see people and what we expect from them. The professional language used by many therapists reveals that they see mental health problems as an indelible part of the people they treat. What is important is that their pessimism may have a negative effect on the person seeking help.

Patients tend to adopt the views of their problems that their therapists hold. So it follows that pessimistic therapists get fewer results than optimistic ones. Those who see problems as unchangeable get fewer changes than those who see problems as only a part of the complex patterns that make people who they are. Research informs us that therapists who talk about the positive and uplifting things that a patient is doing get better results than those who talk only about the problems, the weaknesses, and the shortcomings of patients.

The Uses and Misuses of Diagnoses

It is quite possible that at some time in your work together, your therapist will discuss your condition and treatment, using diagnostic labels that convey a picture to you of your prognosis and ability to change that may be either misleading or at variance with your own perceptions. To recognize what is occurring and correct this tendency, you need to know what diagnoses mean in mental health, their limitations for treatment, and their misuses.

Diagnoses serve these purposes in physical health care:

- They convey information about what causes a condition.
- They convey information about the expected course or prognosis of the condition.

- They convey information about what the appropriate treatment may be.
- They satisfy managed care insurers.

In a less formal way, diagnoses help us step away from the symptoms to see what the real problem is. That is because, in many medical conditions, the overt symptoms may be similar, even though the diagnoses are different. Common symptoms of Parkinson's disease, for example, include a shuffling gait, an inexpressive face, and mutism, the inability to speak. These exact symptoms also can occur as a result of a stroke, Alzheimer's disease, and as a side effect of certain medications. The symptoms do not tell the doctor what the disease is; it only tells her where to look to find the biological dysfunction that must be treated.

Chemical Imbalance and Addiction: The Overuse of a Metaphor

It is popular for doctors who practice medical treatment to explain depression by attributing it to a "chemical imbalance," "genetics," or "neurotransmitter" in the brain. But what does that mean? It also is popular to describe unacceptable and unwanted behaviors as "addictions." We say that people are addicted to love, sex, drugs, gambling, and virtually anything else you can imagine.

In the late nineteenth century, one important theorist posited that for every twisted thought or feeling, there is a twisted molecule in the brain. This may be true, but these twisted molecules have largely defied detection. The chemical imbalances and genes said to "cause" alcoholism, depression, and schizophrenia may be more indicative of how your doctor prefers to think about the problem than they are a reflection of science.

Obviously, while certain severe psychiatric conditions such as schizophrenia have a growing body of evidence to suggest biological and genetic components as part of their origin and course, increasingly terms like "addiction," "chemical imbalance," "genetics," and "neural transmitters" have become catch words that convey the impression that we've actually isolated illnesses and found their visible causes. Identifying such behaviors as gambling, overeating, love, and sex—behaviors that are self-initiated and self-contained—as "addictions" leaves a similar impression—that these behaviors have some stable and clear biological cause. As applied to mental disorders, however, this is a tremendous overstatement. While there is much evidence that a wide variety of behaviors are related to biological conditions and genetic factors, neither the line of demarcation between what is normal type behavior to a biological being nor the direction of causality has been established. In the final analysis, there is little scientific basis for thinking either that most mental health problems actually are diseases rather than extreme variations of normality, or that such activities as gambling, love, sex, and other appetites are addictions. The causal chain between an external substance (such as opioids, alcohol, tobacco) introduced into the body and the presence of physical withdrawal reactions, when such a substance is removed is easy to establish, but such a directional connection is difficult or impossible to establish when one talks of being addicted to one's own behavior. Can one be addicted to one's self? It is troublesome, from a logical perspective, to think of behaviors—things that arise from one's body—as addictions. Is hunger an addiction? Thirst? At what point is a normal desire an addiction and disease, rather than a choice?

Addiction to an outside substance can usefully explain behavior, reduce guilt, and define a correction. When misapplied, it can be an excuse, an avoidance of responsibility, and a rationalization. Applying the concept of an addiction to one's own behavior and appetites (love addiction, sex addiction, and so on) is a metaphor, and an easily overused one.

By calling things "diseases" and "addictions," we imply that these problems are fixable with medicine. These terms perpetuate a myth that is only loosely supported by science. These terms get attention and hold out hope of instant cures. But to call them either chemical imbalances or the causes of behavioral problems is a statement of a belief and hope rather than a fact. When a doctor explains your depression as being a "chemical imbalance," it reflects a model of behavior and belief—the set of working assumptions and values—accepted by your doctor. Your doctor's sociopolitical belief is that all or certain behaviors are reflections of physical disease processes. Other doctors may view the same behaviors from a different set of assumptions and values, one that emphasizes cultural experience and choice.

Certainly, many serious emotional and behavior problems have distinct genetic characteristics, biological patterns, and physical correlates. Sometimes specific genes have been identified, and in other cases the culprit seems to be certain chemical substances. But in science, correlation does not prove causation—just because the chemical substances are present doesn't mean they cause the disorder. They could be a result. In many of these conditions, the causes have remained elusive to researchers.

The unsaid and great mystery for those who view behavior as illness is explaining why most of those who have a designated biology do not have the disorder and why some of those who have the disorder do not have the complementing physiology.

For example, many years ago, a psychiatrist isolated a substance in the blood of schizophrenic individuals that he called Taraxein. He found that if he injected it into normal individuals, they began to hallucinate and develop delusions. Unfortunately, like so many other supposed chemical imbalances before and since, Taraxein proved to be a dead end. Its effects could not be consistently replicated; some evidence indicated that the substance was produced by the patient's behavior rather than vice versa, and still other research suggested that it was a product of a poor diet in the state mental facility where it was first discovered. The research was ultimately abandoned because others could not consistently produce the same result. Unfortunately, most discoveries of supposed chemical imbalances and biological causes of depression and even schizophrenia lack a clear demonstration that these factors are causal rather than consequential.

It may be more helpful to view these biological contributors to mental illness as normal variations of physical functioning across some continuum. Apart from such obviously medical problems as traumatic head injury, toxicity, or neurological conditions such as Parkinson's Disease, there is virtually no way to disentangle contributions from chemicals, genes, and the human experience.

The models therapists use to describe behavioral problems are not inherently "true" or "false." Nor does one set of explanations indicate that the other is incorrect. All behavior is genetically determined in the sense that none can be carried out without the presence of physiologically defined structures and conditions that are part of the human genome. But that does not make aberrant behavior a biological disorder. Likewise, all behavior is subject to environmental constraints and includes elements acquired or learned from experience and training. So in a sense all behaviors are both products of culture and of one's biology.

Culture and Disease

Cultural values can shape even the most basic physiological processes and the most serious behaviors. For example, why do we eat? To say that eating satisfies a biological need is true, but it misses the colorful cultural patterns that characterize our relationship with food. In Western, middle-class cultures, we are not usually deprived of food long enough to experience intense or life-threatening hunger. We eat when we do because it is the norm within our social group, or some particularly tasty food is presented to us. Depending on the culture, however, we do or do not eat meat, we eat once, or twice, or three times a day, we hold the fork in the left or the right hand, we eat at noon or 3:00 P.M., and we have the largest meal of the day at noon or in the evening. Americans may get hungry at six in the evening; Italians may do so at nine. These cultural conventions determine much more of our eating behavior than physical causes of hunger. Our biological and genetic background may determine how easily we become hungry, how fast we metabolize food, and our hunger level. Genetic factors may make us more or less sensitive to food deprivation, but our environment teaches us how to cope with it, when we should eat, and when it's not acceptable to eat.

If our biological inheritance sets our bodies to be very reactive to short periods of food deprivation, inducing widely varying changes in blood glucose levels over just a few hours, what we have learned culturally may not fit our needs. We may need to eat more frequently than is conventional, or we may be drawn to different foods than is "normal." These are legitimate variations, they are not diseases. Imagine the implications of defining as a "disease" every biological quality that doesn't quite fit the usual pattern within a culture. Would a person experiencing extreme hunger at noon be considered to have a "disease" in a culture that didn't eat until four or five?

The role of culture in mental and emotional problems can also be seen in the extreme example of suicide, a behavior that our Western society considers one of the most serious consequences of a mental disorder. In some cultures, suicide attempts are often characteristic of groups of individuals who are dependent for their well-being on powerful institutions or persons. In those situations making a suicide attempt is felt to be one of the few acts that will mobilize or influence others to take notice of one's grievances.

While many Western mental health authorities believe that suicide is primarily related to a major psychiatric disease (the most common being a depressive illness), some other cultures see suicide as a normal and accepted response to being a repressed minority or being socially embarrassed. In Western culture, 90 percent of all those who commit suicide had a diagnosable psychiatric illness (primarily depression, alcoholism, or schizophrenia).

While much of the data on suicide is based on information obtained from developed Western societies that share a Judeo-Christian heritage, which regards suicide as a sin, there are clear cultural variations in how suicide is viewed and when suicide impulses need treatment. For example, in the Aguarana, a people along the Peruvian Amazon, the high rate of suicide is seen as part of a complex social process that links death threats, homicide, assertions of personal autonomy, and relations to dominance with an individual's inability to be part of a collective response to interpersonal conflict. Female suicides are particularly common.

The local explanation for these suicides—from the Aguarana men—is that women lack the ability to control strong emotions. Yet there is no question that women's oppressed position is also fraught with ambivalence. In a study of American suicidal women and their relationships to husbands, boyfriends, or lovers, the suicide attempt often simultaneously represented a flight from an unhappy, sometimes physically violent, relationship and a desperate attempt to restore it on a different footing.

Suicide can also be a logical reaction to a traditional system of beliefs about gender. For example, among the Gainj, inhabitants of the highlands of Papua, New Guinea, female suicide is considered a viable option when women keep their part of the relationship or gender bargain and men do not.

And, there is a long tradition in Japanese culture of taking one's own life when honor has been compromised.

A Consolidated View of Treatment

Why are some people unhappy? There are probably many reasons—they may be coping with some type of loss, their family may have taught unhappiness in indirect ways, temperament that is genetically transmitted may predispose them to very low or high emotional sensitivity and vibrancy, they may have learned the consequences of engaging in depressed behaviors, and so on.

The biological and environmental forces that shape unhappiness vary from person to person in how they affect behavior. So it is very difficult to disentangle the contributions made by biology and those made by social forces. Moreover, it is arbitrary and misleading to do so. In our effort to avoid minimizing the importance of emotional problems, we (as a Western culture) have come to include many normal variations from average behavior in our system of classifying diseases. We may have come to a point that in order to avoid overreacting to these problems, we must reduce our overreliance on a disease metaphor to explain behavior in more personally responsible terms.

If we talk solely of biological "causes," the suggestion is that the use of medical treatments, like Prozac and Xanax, is most appropriate. While if we look at solely environmental "causes," we may value treatments that include only psychosocial interventions, such as psychotherapy, education, and environmental change. In the cases of schizophrenia and some bipolar disorders, however, there is evidence that treatment with drugs is preferable, but for many other disorders that afflict us, there is no evidence that drugs work better than psychotherapy. What is important is whether the therapist's view of "cause" and treatment fits yours.

In other words, the critical issue may not be whether the explanation given by your doctor or therapist is correct, technically speaking, but whether you are prepared to believe it. Benefit may correlate with the degree to which the nature of the treatment you get fits your value system: Do you prefer to think of your behavior as arising from a disease, or from the lack of skills necessary to cope with and adapt to stress?

Medications to make you feel better and counseling to help you learn and grow will be helpful for most problems, in various degrees. But the relative value of any of these treatments is less founded in some basic truth about the basis of mental and emotional problems and is more a reflection of the beliefs and value systems you—and your therapist—hold. These treatments, like the diseases they are designed to address, are reflections of our culture.

GUIDELINES TO KEEP IN MIND

The use of labels in the form of diagnoses in health care is conventional and has a number of advantages or potential advantages.

* A diagnosis provides a shorthand description of important behaviors that are disruptive or self-defeating.
* A diagnosis allows insurance and other third-party payers to justify payment.
* A diagnosis reduces unnecessary and nonproductive guilt and self-blame for one's behavior.
* A diagnosis offers a way of understanding and making sense of one's experiences and problems.
* A diagnosis suggests some helpful treatment directions.

Despite these advantages, we have identified several potential negative consequences of applying diagnostic labels. Among them:

* There may be a tendency to treat these explanations as factual when they are not.
* Labels may overemphasize the concept of pathology—that you have an illness—and minimize the normal and adaptive functions of that behavior.

* Labels dictate a form of treatment that may be incompatible with or ineffective for you.
* Labels may mislead you to think that the causes of a problem can be known, are an indelible part of the person, or are unchangeable.
* Labels may overshadow a focus on important strengths and assets that characterize you.
* Labels may help you avoid taking responsibility for changing your behavior and denying the consequences of that behavior.

When your doctor suggests a diagnosis for your complaint, ask questions. Don't be afraid of talking to your therapist about your diagnosis. If it doesn't make sense to you, say so.

* Keep in mind that most explanations are tentative and that most behaviors have multiple causes.
* Ask your therapist or doctor if there are other possible causes and treatments besides those mentioned.
* Don't just accept a label—few things are certain or written in stone. It is your right and responsibility to make sure that you both understand your therapist's formulation and agree with the treatment.
* If the proposed treatment is not compatible or acceptable, seek a second opinion and consider finding another course of treatment. Don't forget that a second opinion is always an option and a right when you disagree with the diagnosis and descriptions given to you.

Protection from the potential misuses of labels comes through a knowledge of the different models that direct therapists' treatments, the nature of the treatments that derive from these models, and the scientific status of these treatments. We look at these topics next.

6

⚭

What Is Different
About Different
Therapies?

Timothy J was about to get married. His fiancée, Brenda was a strong young woman, bright and ambitious, while Timothy tended to be quiet and unadventurous. Nonetheless, they were in love and their attributes seemed to compliment one another. But as soon as Brenda set the date for marriage, Timothy's life turned upside down. At times he couldn't breath, feeling as if he were having a heart attack. The fear prevented him from doing his work, making love, even sleeping.

Brenda decided Timothy needed some help and sought out a counselor at a local family service agency. They talked about their families and Timothy's feelings about himself and his relationship with his mother. The counselor told Timothy he would need individual psychotherapy with her. But as each week passed, Timothy continued to get worse. After a frantic late-night telephone call from Brenda, the counselor sent Timothy to an internist who prescribed large amounts of Valium. Still Timothy continued to get worse. He was in danger of losing his job, and Brenda was berating him for what was happening with their relationship.

Finally, one day at lunch, Timothy confided to a friend the disaster his life had become. His friend referred him to a behavioral psychologist who concluded he had a textbook case of panic attack, and referred him to an anxiety disorder clinic at a nearby university where he went through a well-validated cognitive-behavioral treatment protocol. The clinic's psychiatrist immediately changed his medication to Xanax, and after four weeks of therapy, Timothy began feeling better. By ten weeks, he was free of symptoms. He and Brenda are now happily married and he is in business for himself.

Again, a patient needing help didn't get it because he went to the wrong person who prescribed the wrong therapy for his problems. Practitioners, as we've seen, are a very mixed group and the nature of the treatments they offer is equally varied. The variability among treatments partly reflects the widely diverse theories that characterize clinical practice.

These theories, while formally structured and accepted within a given school, are largely lacking in external evidence of validity, and are always limited and incomplete. They are working "theories" that dictate how patients should be treated by those who share this view. This chapter will explore some of these theories, their evolution and contemporary development, and their implications for what you may experience when you seek help for your emotional distress.

In this chapter, we will review the major models or theories that guide treatment in the domain of mental health. B. F. Skinner, the noted behavioral psychologist, referred to theories as convenient fictions. This is a captivating characterization and it underscores the fact that all theories are partly myth, combined with fact and hope. Their value is that they help us predict and control events in our lives. All people use theories. The only thing that makes our day-to-day theories different from formal ones is how explicit they are. Here, we will describe the major explicit theories that are used to explain, predict, and control behavior. This will serve as a background for our discussion of who can benefit the most from these different theories.

Contemporary Theories in Mental Health

To predict behavior and control consequences, people use theories of personality. A theory is a mental model, outline, or framework constructed from the assumptions and beliefs that we have about what controls and predicts behavior.

Today there are more than 400 different explicit and formal theories of behavior used to guide contemporary mental health treatment. Clearly, it is unlikely that there is one that is "true" at the exclusion of the rest. Moreover, it is unlikely that even if one theory is factually more correct than the others, it cannot be demonstrated scientifically. Theories can be productive and helpful, even if their validity cannot or has not been clearly demonstrated. Their value is not in their truth, but in the degree to which they help people overcome unhappiness.

While finding the truth of a theory is of interest to scientists, the most important question that you, as a patient in mental health treatment, must address is not "Which theory is right?" but "Which theory will be sufficiently compatible with my own view of life and will help me grow?"

In the service of helping you address that question, this chapter will review some of the major contemporary theories and describe briefly what you can expect of a therapist who adopts each of these theories. From our descriptions, we hope you can find a theoretical perspective that is compatible with what you value and that is associated with a therapist's methods that fit your preferences.

We review five general theories, each embodying a different set of assumptions and values. Many of the more than 400 theories are variations on these five viewpoints. They are:

- Psychodynamic models
- Behavioral and cognitive-behavioral models
- Humanistic-experiential models
- Interpersonal-systems models
- Biological models

These models of behavior are sometimes given different names than those used here, but the ideas are the same. We look at how the different theories explain the causes of your problems and view the treatments each uses.

Psychodynamic Models

"Psychodynamic" theories propose that inner conflict is a primary motivator of behavior as well as the generator of psychiatric symptoms. Most psychodynamic theories generally have evolved from Freud's system of psychoanalysis.

Sigmund Freud's ideas have permeated our world in many ways, both obvious and subtle. It is safe to say that Freud and his approach to psychoanalysis are still what many laypeople think of when they speak of psychology and psychotherapy. The story of psychoanalysis began when a physician, Josef Breuer, in the last decade of the nineteenth century told Freud about a remarkable experience he was having with a patient who seemed to be curing herself of the symptoms of hysteria by simply talking about them. Breuer had observed that when this patient was put into a hypnotic trance, she often would become emotional and report a highly charged emotional event. Subsequent to this hypnotic episode, she appeared relieved of her symptoms.

Freud came to the conclusion that the traumatic events involved in causing hysteria took place in childhood and were usually of a sexual nature. The task of therapy was seen as bringing about the recollection of the forgotten events together with a cathartic release of repressed emotions.

The second phase of Freud's discoveries revolved around his search to unravel the riddle of dreams. Dreams and symptoms, Freud came to believe, had a similar structure. They were both the end-product of a compromise between two sets of opposing forces in the mind—unconscious sexual wishes seeking discharge, on the one hand, and the repressive activity of the overly socialized mind, on the other. Both a dream element and a symptom represented a disguised wish, a hidden compromise worked out by the unconscious mind between the impulses (the *id*) and the social conscience (*superego*). When these two forces, both driven by unconscious and unrealistic desires or demands, confronted the real world, a realistic aspect of consciousness arose—the *ego*. Freud postulated that this conscious structure guided and directed everyday behavior by mediating between the forces of id and superego. This behavior, however, always included unrealistic perceptions, and when either the id's or superego's demands became dominant, the result was a "neurosis." Freud's method of discovery was through careful anecdotal observations, a method of investigation that would not earn the respect of many modern scientists.

One of Freud's early patients, Paul Lorenz, illustrates Freud's concept of conflict and his belief that the roots of neurosis lay in unresolved, early, but unrealistic sexual fantasies. Lorenz, a man suffering from obsessive fears that something terrible was going to happen to his father, was so burdened by his obsessive thoughts about his father's well-being that he developed ritualized compulsive behaviors to ward off this harm, became extremely anxious, lost sexual potency, and was unable to complete work on his law degree. His worries were decidedly peculiar since his father had been dead for years.

Freud believed that Lorenz had not successfully resolved the oedipal conflict. The oedipal conflict arose, according to Freud, from the male child's desire to seduce his mother. The child was inevitably faced with the fear that if his father were to discover these intentions, the child would be castrated or put to death—a decidedly disturbing prospect. In normal development, Freud proposed that the child would, in a forced compromise, transfer his illicit strivings to a symbolic form. He would identify with his father to maintain a vicarious sexual relationship with mother, and ultimately to redirect his sexual energies to finding a mother substitute—a wife.

Freud saw the fears of Lorenz as reflecting the love–hate dynamic of these oedipal struggles, and because Lorenz repressed but never really gave up on his incestuous desires, brought his fears into adulthood as an obsessional neurosis. The hostile feelings and jealousies that he experienced toward his father were unacceptable to him and were repressed by the ego, pushing their way to the surface in the form of obsessions that symbolically represented his fear that his impulses would (or had) caused his father's death.

Psychoanalytic theory assumes that events in the mind are not random, haphazard unrelated phenomena. The thoughts, feelings, and impulses that come into awareness—including mistakes, slips of the tongue—are events in a chain of causally related phenomena in which unconscious impulses from the id leak into everyday behaviors. The idea that all events and behaviors are caused by mental events is called "psychic determinism." By analyzing the connection between the current mental experience and both past and current events, recovery from repression was thought to be achieved, producing "insight" and cure.

A second principle of psychoanalysis is the assumption that mental events exist along a continuum of consciousness. Events of which we are aware constitute the conscious mind. Events that are outside our awareness but are readily recalled with concentration make up the preconscious mind. The *unconscious mind* consists of events that cannot be recalled because they have been protectively forced out of awareness and repressed. The unconscious is the engine of behavior. It is maintained by repression, and repression is an active persistent process that motivates behavior and stops an individual from thinking or knowing about—or even being aware of—motives, feelings, and external events that threaten to expose id-based drives, particularly sexual wishes (*libido*).

The third of Freud's principles defines how we store and move energy. Freud assumed that each person has a finite amount of energy allotted by his or her biological inheritance. This energy is generated by the id as sexual and aggressive urges, and because these impulses are unacceptable to the superego, they are channeled from one activity to another in a dynamic process. The ego controls the movement and channeling of this energy. It activates the mind to do work and the body to act.

The fourth principle of psychoanalysis is embodied in psychosexual development. This principle asserts that conflicts arise as sequential stages during early life; failure to resolve these conflicts produces a fixation and ensures that these conflicts will contaminate subsequent behaviors and perceptions. The intrusion of the past on the present produces neurotic symptoms and character traits.

Freud organized developmental experience into several phases that he termed oral (approximately from birth to two years of age), anal (from about ages two to four), phallic (from ages four to six), and, later, genital (adulthood), each expressing the bodily system through which one is likely to express sexual impulses.

On mental trauma, psychoanalytic theory asserted that any individual who finds him or herself, in adult life, facing a situation that is similar to the one in which the original trauma was experienced would unrealistically reenact the original experience. Reenactment was considered the product of filtering experience through the now-repressed memories of the childhood conflict, making the individual respond as he or she did in childhood.

However expansively Freud constructed his psychology, and no matter how ambitious his ultimate aims might have been, he seemed to be aware that his theory was a construct beyond the scope of scientific methods. He often was cautious about the nature of his findings.

Yet, at other times, he seemed to externalize and intensify the belief in his views and resented those who challenged the theory. He was notorious for his rejection of former friends and colleagues who deserted or challenged his views. Carl Jung and Alfred Adler were two who broke with Freud in 1911 and 1913 and earned his life-long enmity. Jung disagreed with Freud about the nature of drives, and Adler rejected Freud's emphasis on the id as the basis for motivated behavior.

Traditional psychoanalysis evolving from Freud made use of a long-term intensive series of introspective sessions in which the patient faced away from the analyst or reclined on a couch. Except for the emphasis in contemporary applications on reducing the length of therapy and frequency of sessions, the psychoanalytic session today is conducted in a manner very similar to Freud's practice. It includes the use of the couch, free association as the primary technique, interpretations of dreams and fantasies by the analyst, an impersonal and neutral attitude on the part of the analyst, and the interpretative analysis of recurring patterns in relationships, particularly as they are manifest in the psychotherapy relationship itself.

Freud first used hypnosis to induce insight, but quickly abandoned this procedure in favor of the method of "free association." The patient was invited to speak freely, expressing any thought that passed through his or her mind, and without withholding anything that might come to consciousness. Interpretations by the analyst accompanied the process of free association. Interpretations suggested a meaning to the topics, identified the assumed wishes that underlay these ramblings, described the conflicts assumed to be driving behavior, and confronted the defenses that the patient erected against insight. This process would force repressed material to slowly work its way into consciousness and undermine the symptoms.

In contemporary psychodynamic practice, few psychotherapists see their patients more than four times a week. Freud saw patients five and six times weekly. This change partially reflects the refusal of managed health care systems to support such intensive practices as well as a declining interest in this form of treatment by patients.

While all psychodynamic derivatives of psychoanalysis assert the importance of conflict as the basis of behavior, contemporary theories differ in what they consider the nature of this conflict. Psychoanalysis, as classically formulated by Freud, for example, identified the impulses that were at the root of conflict as being sexual and aggressive. More modern developments include theories that view these impulses as more neutral, capable of being channeled in either negative or positive ways. Potentially, for example, the self-centered reflections can result in enhanced self-worth and a sense of personal regard and power if properly channeled. Freud viewed sexual impulses as inherently destructive, but the modified, modern views consider such positive qualities as self-esteem to also arise from these self-directed sexual drives.

A therapist who works from a psychodynamic model of behavior usually makes three basic assumptions in treatment:

- That change comes from understanding or insight into the nature of one's conflicts.
- That the most dominant conflicts that produce problems for which one seeks treatment are likely to be enacted in some form in the perceptions of and reactions to the therapist.
- That effective treatment consists of a "corrective emotional experience"—in other words, the nurturing qualities that were missing from early relationships are provided in the safety of the therapy relationship.

Most therapists using psychodynamic theory tend to be relatively inactive in the therapy hour; they seldom offer suggestions and are frequently silent, preferring to let people find their own way and set their own directions. They may ask you to say out loud whatever comes to mind, describe dreams and fantasies, or examine feelings. Those who employ more structure may talk more, may direct your attention to different experiences that may have occurred in your past, and may even provide some suggestions and recommendations.

Some therapists have attempted to shorten the process of therapy by restricting their focus to recent events. These theorists focus specifically on exploring the manifestation and meaning of conflicts that occur and recur in one's significant relationships instead of directing attention to such intrapsychic processes as sexual instincts or general aggressive impulses. This places the nature of the conflicts within a context that includes others and diminishes some of the criticisms suggesting that psychodynamic theories ignore the context in which behavior occurs.

Freud's personal history played a major role in how he viewed the world, and his family life, prejudices, and religion all were integral parts of what became psychoanalysis. Unfortunately, this self-focus deprived Freud of objectivity, a concern perpetuated in later theoretical modifications by the frequent failure to put in place external validity checks on therapist's interpretations.

As a result of this lack of objectivity, a number of criticisms have been leveled at psychodynamic thought. The most persistent and influential was launched by behavioral researchers and it emphasized lack of precision of concepts and objective evidence in tests of psychoanalytic theory.

Behavioral and Cognitive-Behavioral Models

Behaviorism constituted the second major wave in the history of modern psychological treatments. In the early part of this century, the distinguished Russian physiologist, Ivan Pavlov, began his well-known studies of what he called "conditioning" (we may also call it "learning"), using dogs as his subjects. If you put meat in a dog's mouth, the dog will salivate. Pavlov discovered that if a stimulus such as a bell, tone, or light were presented immediately before inserting the meat a few times, the dog learned to salivate even without meat. In other words, the dog had learned to salivate when the bell sounded. On one hand, the observation that dogs will learn to salivate when a new object becomes associated with food was hardly remarkable—everyone who has fed dogs knows that. But the systematic measurement and scientific rigor applied to this demonstration gave new meaning and significance to the observation. It opened new avenues for studying a decidedly human activity, the acquisition of behavior.

Pavlov's work also had significance for understanding how things are unlearned. If the experimenter stopped giving meat in association with the bell signal, the dog would gradually stop salivating at the sound of the bell. The procedure of withholding the "conditioned" stimulus came to be called "extinction."

J. B. Watson was a strong advocate of "radical behaviorism," and believed that Pavlov's laws of "classical conditioning" could explain fears and personality traits. Together with his student P. Raynor, they conducted a now famous experiment on an eleven-month-old boy named Albert to demonstrate how emotional problems could be lessened.

Albert had a quiet, easygoing disposition and appeared to be fearless. In the first stage of the experiment, Albert was shown a white rat, a rabbit, a dog, and cotton, and was allowed to play with them. To introduce a fear-inducing unconditioned stimulus, Watson and Raynor made a sudden, loud, and unpleasant noise by banging a steel bar when Albert came in contact with a white rat. In the first session the bar was struck on two occasions when Albert reached out to touch the rat. A week later they did it five more times. On the eighth trial they showed the boy the rat alone, and he immediately began to cry and crawl away rapidly. Five days later they tested Albert for generalization of the fear response. He played as usual with wooden blocks showing no signs of fear. When they put the rabbit in front of him, he leaned away, whimpered, and finally burst out into tears. Albert showed similar, though not as strong reactions to the dog, cotton, a fur coat, and even the experimenter's hair—examples of "stimulus generalization."

Albert had acquired a phobia of white furry animals by a simple conditioning process, and from these experiments the researchers assumed we could learn how we acquired many human fears that seem irrational and puzzling. Fear of heights or fear of snakes were explained by the laws of learning, by accidental conditioning that paired unconditioned and conditioned stimuli, and by subsequent generalization.

"Operant conditioning," developed by the noted psychologist B. F. Skinner, contrasts with classical conditioning in its focus on the consequences of complex behaviors rather than on simple association. In this view, feelings and behaviors occur because of the history of how those close to you respond to your behavior, how they've responded in the past, the likelihood of incurring a similar response in the present, and the frequency of prior reinforcement.

Skinner determined that people and other animals learn to make a response when doing so produces some favorable consequence. This consequence is called a "reinforcer." Behaviors followed by a desirable event (positive reinforcer), or by the termination of an undesirable one (negative reinforcer), persisted. Moreover, the longer the time in which a behavior has been reinforced, the more durable it is.

There are some peculiarities to the concept of reinforcement, however. Most specifically, it is assumed that a behavior will develop most rapidly if the positive or negative reinforcement is consistent and predictable. But the behavior is maintained longer and is less tractable if the reinforcement—positive or negative—has become unpredictable and inconsistent. This is especially true for the case of a behavior that arises from negative reinforcement, which includes the most problematic and destructive feelings and behaviors.

Contemporary behavioral models have modified and extended the original ideas of Pavlov and Skinner. Three particularly noteworthy ones—radical behaviorism, social learning theory, and cognitive therapy—demonstrate the varieties of values and assumptions that guide behavior therapists. The first emphasizes the role of environmental contingencies on behaviors that are observable. The second highlights the power of imitation and social reward in changing behavior. The third emphasizes the importance of thoughts in producing behaviors.

Treatment from a radical behaviorist viewpoint involves identifying the ways in which unhappy feelings are manifest in overt behavior. This includes determining how certain behaviors may interrupt your ability to work or carry on desired life activities. Sometimes, this means identifying the anticipated negative consequences that keep you from behaving in desirable ways; other times it means simply identifying the consequences that accrue after either positive or negative behavior.

You can expect the radical behavior therapist to take an active role in defining the problem and suggesting solutions. You keep records, chart your activities, identify feared and desired events, practice engaging in feared behaviors in new situations while you assess the consequences, and rehearse new behaviors in old circumstances.

The social learning approach falls somewhere in between a psychodynamic approach and a radical behavior approach. For example, some psychologists retain the basic models of classical and operant conditioning but also accept internal events as possible controlling stimuli and as possible sources of self-reinforcement.

Treatment in this system of thought rests on the assumption that troubled people do things that reduce their chances of receiving positive reinforcements. For example, they may withdraw from social activities and thus reduce the possibility that they will receive social support, find love, or receive acceptance. Treatment focuses on creating situations in which they can again enjoy the rewards of social and intimate relationships. If treated in this way, you might be encouraged to do more things that once produced pleasure, to seek out more social enjoyments, and to benefit from watching how others handle difficult situations and succeed. Keeping records and carrying out homework assignments are important characteristics of this treatment.

Cognitive therapies are the most recent additions to the therapists' repertoire. These theories question the simplicity of behavior theory, arguing that it gives inadequate attention to mental events and information processing. They focus on processes that mediate, or intervene, between the environment and the behavior or feeling that is the problem.

If a person has learned to expect failure, becomes confused, is afraid, or views herself as ineffective, she may be likely to do poorly, develop negative self-images, and withdraw from social environments. All these behaviors are symptoms of depression. Depressed persons in this view have learned to regard themselves as ineffective and unworthy.

These theories propose that when individuals are confronted by a situation, they appraise that stimulus in light of their memories, beliefs, and expectations before reacting. What determines the response is not the situation itself, but the person's interpretation of it. They suggest that people control their behavior to a larger extent than they are aware. This is for good or ill. Many disturbed and dysfunctional behaviors, as well as success in coping with difficulties, are traceable to the things people say to themselves, approvingly or disapprovingly, about their abilities to interact or cope with the environment. According to this interpretation, repression is a behavioral representation of an attitude of hopelessness.

Those who use cognitive models of behavior tend to focus on both the methods a patient uses to solve problems and the different forms that assumptions may take when bad and good events occur. Most share two fundamental beliefs about what we need to correct problems. They assume that patients will benefit from learning to accurately appraise the truth of their beliefs. They also believe that a systematic method of instruction and practice will correct inaccurate knowledge and deficiencies in information processing.

Considerable variations exist among cognitive and behavioral therapists in how they address and implement these assumptions. However, one can ordinarily expect that the therapist will be relatively active, will set fairly straightforward goals, and will give you or help you construct homework assignments. These assignments will include monitoring situations and the responses that give you problems, having you keep track of your activities, and asking you to practice new thoughts and behaviors. Indeed, the idea of homework is so deeply ingrained in this model that if you don't get such assignments, you should probably ask the therapist why the therapy is not being followed in the usual fashion.

Humanistic-Experiential Models

To some, the behavioral reaction to the looseness of psychoanalytic thought went too far. Shortly after behavioristic models took root, other reactions to them occurred. One emphasized the importance of reconnecting with the spiritual, with inner experience, and with the equality of humankind. The humanistic-experiential view objected to the failure of both psychoanalytic and behavioral therapies to connect with authentic "feeling."

The survivors of the Holocaust during World War II reminded the world of the power of inner commitment. They proved that the worst possible experience could be overcome by finding a meaning in existence that extended beyond one's immediate situation. Humanistic and experiential approaches to psychotherapy were born of this awareness. Viktor Frankl, one of these survivors, is credited with bringing an understanding of these inner resources to emerging theories of psychotherapy.

The resulting collection of theories that arose from this understanding holds three beliefs in common:

- The belief in an inherent growth-oriented process, often referred to as "self-actualization."
- The belief that emotional and sensory experiences are inherently good, but are suppressed by a society that is fearful of strong emotions.
- The belief that growth forces are made active by unencumbered emotional expression.

To release the forces of growth, an environment was needed that was supportive of self-determination, permissive of strong feelings, and open to new experiences. The structure and setting of psychotherapy were to provide such an environment.

The growth potential assigned to people by the humanistic-experiential school contrasted with the role of victim that was assigned by psychodynamic models, and the value assigned to inner experience contrasted with the value placed on overt experience by the behaviorists.

Humanistic-experiential theories believed that a natural and inherent drive directed the growth and development of each person's potential, a drive called "self-actualization." This school of thought asserted that everyone is inherently able to reorganize their experiences to overcome emotional pain, depression, and unhappiness.

While rising to prominence after World War II, experiential treatment had its origins in the European existential philosophies of Søren Kierkegaard, Jean Paul Sartre, Edmund Husserl, and Martin

Heidegger. Existentialism describes the conditions of modern humanity, with particular emphasis on feelings of loneliness, alienation, and isolation that incapacitate a person and leave one incapable of action. Perhaps of greatest significance historically is that by attending to the depersonalization and isolation of modern humanity in relation with others, the existential approach came to fill a real void. It asked very basic and important questions, and developed a core of basic human values not fully realized in the other schools of therapy.

Even in its therapeutic applications, this existential approach concentrates on the philosophical assumptions that underlie therapy rather than on the techniques of therapy. Of all the therapies, the experiential psychotherapies were designed to focus almost exclusively on crucial questions about the nature of humanity. The treatment and its answers are sometimes poetic, often confusing, and usually stimulating.

Modern renditions of humanistic-experiential therapies embody assumptions that are similar to psychodynamic models. They assume that problematic behaviors and symptoms have internal causes, that these causes are enduring sources of conflict, and that symptoms represent a compromise in which reductions of anxiety are purchased by ignoring, suppressing, or denying these conflictual experiences.

There are also differences. Experiential theories point to emotion as the primary experience that is excluded, while psychodynamic theories target repressed mental events and impulses. Experiential schools emphasize that the road to cure is awareness of feelings and sensations, while psychodynamic theories see insight into one's motives as inherent in the healing process. Finally, and perhaps most important, humanistic-experiential schools see the primary human impulse to express emotions as growth enhancing, while psychodynamic models view these impulses as inherently destructive.

Carl Rogers, the leading light in the extension of humanistic-experiential thought to American psychotherapy, believed that for psychotherapy to succeed, the therapist must come to understand the patient so completely that the theorist becomes a virtual alter ego.

It is this warm willingness on the part of the counselor to lay aside his/her own self temporarily, in order to enter into the experience of the patient, that makes the relationship a completely unique one, unlike anything in the patient's previous experience.

The other crucial aspect of the relationship to Rogers was the emphasis on providing safety and security for the patient. It was a central tenet that the therapist must create an environment in which the patient will be accepted, and judgmental criticism withheld along with both probing of hidden motives and interpretation of one's personality.

The most essential criticism of Roger's patient-centered approach has been that it can only be effective if the patients do indeed have all the knowledge and skill needed to make important decisions and to change their lives. While Rogers, like others in the humanistic-experiential movement, valued subjective over objective experience, he can be credited with bringing sound empirical methods to bear on the study of therapeutic processes and outcomes.

Interpersonal-Systems Models

Interpersonal schools of thought assume that no behavior occurs in a vacuum. All behavior is a reflection of a social system and is a response to other people. Interpersonal-systems models of disturbed behavior emphasize that the social system one identifies with—usually the family—is goal oriented and dynamic. Its strategic goal is usually unconscious but revolves around the maintenance of a static balance of power and a sense of well-being (albeit a false one) among members.

Some variations on this theme emphasize that families operate as units, with a division of responsibility, including the responsibility of keeping the family unaware of problems. A family equivalent of repression is thought to be one way of maintaining equilibrium by channeling all problems through one family member who becomes the "symptom bearer." This way of maintaining the semblance of health in a dysfunctional family is to covertly appoint one member to draw attention away from family problems by developing some serious behavioral disturbances of his or her own. Of course, all of these permutations and dynamics are carried out unconsciously;

the family has collectively repressed the real conflict and threat.

This theory bears certain similarities to psychodynamic theories and therefore confronts the same problems. It poses a theory that is impossible to validate—if you could be aware of the repressed impulse, it would not be repressed. The evidence for the theory rests on the very behaviors that are being explained. In an interpersonal psychotherapy model (IPT) that attempts to circumvent these theoretical weaknesses, a variety of emotional problems—drug abuse, anxiety, eating disorders—are thought to derive from one or more of four basic interpersonal processes:

- Grieving the loss of people or social activities that have given one a sense of purpose
- Failing to develop adequate interpersonal skills
- Making difficult social role transitions
- Confronting interpersonal conflicts or disputes

IPT includes procedures for determining through independent means, which of these processes lies at the basis of your problems. Moreover, the therapy is described in ways that can be validated independently of the theory itself.

The nature of treatment within an interpersonal model varies. Often the treatment includes people who are part of the system (usually the family) rather than just the patient. Family members are encouraged to see the problems of any one member as reflections of the interplay of everyone else. A child who is disruptive and aggressive may be drawing attention from parents who argue all the time. Refocusing parental conflict on the child's problems may give the family a reason to stay together.

In this specific form of IPT treatment, therapists teach patients that their depression or anxiety is a "disease" that is caused by no act of their own, and that improvement depends on their ability to assume a "sick role," giving in to the recommendations and expertise of their doctor. The patient is taught to view and explore these external events and is encouraged to allow normal processes of "healing" to take place.

If you are in this type of treatment, you can expect to discuss current relationships in your life, identify individuals and social situations you have difficulties with, and, frequently, take medication. Above all, you will be encouraged to accept the therapist's expertise and to rest and observe the natural processes of recovery.

The recovery process will vary somewhat depending on the nature of the problem identified; grief, the processes of role transition, and interpersonal disputes are factors most directly thought to be self-healing. The absence of adaptive social skills, however, sometimes requires a more active approach, with the therapist instructing the patient in the methods of problem solving, or self-assertion, and so on. Sometimes, you may be encouraged to bring a significant other with whom conflicts have occurred to a session. At these times, you and the other person may be asked to engage in role-playing activities or to discuss and agree upon a solution to your difficulties.

Biological Models

Some theories of emotional problems view behavior as a reflection of true physical "illnesses." We have discussed some aspects and implication of these models in preceding chapters. It is important to underscore, however, that biological models place great faith in applying diagnoses. These labels and associated symptom clusters are assumed to reflect actual dysfunctions in and breakdowns of normal biological processes. The causes of behavior are attributed to

- A genetic history
- Disordered neural transmitter systems
- Alterations of bodily secretions
- Structural changes in the brain and nervous system

Variations on this biological theme place different emphases on these different but related processes. To say that the source of behavior is "in the genes," however, does not imply—even to the most staunch genetic purist—that behavior is either unchangeable or unaffected by environment and experience. Genetic histories are used to identify "risk" factors, or the range of behaviors that can be expected in different environments, rather than propose indelible indicators of inevitable disease.

Children of parents who are schizophrenic, alcoholic, or bipolar, for example, are much more likely to develop these conditions than other children, even when they have been raised apart from their disturbed parents. The actual likelihood of having one of these conditions is still quite small, even if a close family member has the diagnosed disorder. Yet the risk of succumbing to that particular disorder is increased. This is an example of a "specific risk."

In other cases, the genetic history does not identify a specific risk, but a general one. It determines a general risk of becoming symptomatic but not having the specific nature of the symptoms. For example, unlike alcoholism or schizophrenia, a family history of anxiety disorders does not increase the likelihood of a family member having the same disorder or even the same class of disorder. It does increase the likelihood of having some emotional problem and of receiving a psychiatric diagnosis at some time in the future.

Instead of looking to genes, some biological theorists explain disruptions to behavior and feelings as disturbances in the release or production of neurotransmitter substances in the brain. These substances normally facilitate or inhibit the transmission of electrochemical impulses across the "synapse" or space between nerve cells, which are called neurons. They emphasize that all behaviors involve a coordinated pattern of transmission between neurons. Some neurons cease to fire, while others fire in a coordinated fashion.

Chemicals that facilitate the transmission of electrochemical impulses from one neuron to another, or others that stop, slow, or inhibit neurons from firing, must be available at any specific receptor site in the neurons. Disrupted neural circuitry may be a product of (1) the lack of neurotransmitter at the point of neural transmission, (2) depletion of the substance that removes the neurotransmitter once it is expended, (3) too many or too few receptors that receive incoming electrochemical impulses, thus blocking the ability of the various neurotransmitter to build a bridge, and (4) damaged neurons that impede transmission. Some cases of depression, as well as Alzheimer's, Parkinson's disease, and other disorders, are related to changes in one or more of these processes.

Usually, when a therapist talks about a "chemical imbalance," he or she is talking about disruptions to the neurotransmitter. However, those aren't the only possibilities. Changes in the body's ability to process glucose or carbohydrates and accompanying changes in blood and oxygen flow to the brain, the production of toxins, the overproduction of brain stimulants, and altered balance or flow of hormones are also among the biological events that sometimes are thought to be causes of disordered behavior.

Still other theorists believe that damage to specific structures in the brain, incurred by unknown trauma or exposure to environmental toxins, account for many forms of disrupted behaviors. These are the most speculative theories when applied to such general symptoms as depression and anxiety, but they certainly account for specific behavioral problems that follow injury or drug abuse.

Therapists who accept any of these biological models as primary explanations of life's problems are likely to urge the use of medications and sometimes even such medical procedures as surgery to correct the problems.

Beyond their common reliance on biological explanations and medication, however, many variations exist among theorists in how they incorporate nonbiological explanations into their explanations and treatment. Many hold to both a biological model and a psychodynamic, or behavioral model, at the same time. Others only accept certain pieces of one or another biological model.

For example, some therapists think that biological causes explain only certain behaviors and not others, so they prescribe medication for some symptoms and psychotherapy for others. Others separate their beliefs of cause from those related to treatment: They view the treatments that derive from biological research as useful, even if the assumptions of biological causes are inaccurate. These therapists may recommend the use of medications as a way of reducing symptoms, but still deny a belief in the primacy of biological explanations of behavior and feelings.

GUIDELINES TO KEEP IN MIND

This short review of major theories reveals the wide variety of speculations about what causes, and cures, various disorders. The lack of certainty and "truth" that pervades this field are clearly evident. While theorists of any ilk often sound assured, certain, and logical in describing the cause of your problems, remember that all these explanations are based on theories, some on factual data, and some quite speculative. There is no model that can clearly brag to have risen above all others in pointing to a substantial body of evidence that supports its superiority.

There are, however, some models that have failed to generate strong scientific support. Usually, these are the more complex theories, and it is uncertain whether the lack of support is because the theories are invalid or because they are simply too difficult to subject to scientific tests by the usual methods.

We have already commented on the weak scientific evidence available for psychodynamic and some systems theories. However, both models have generated a body of support for the effectiveness of their treatment, at least as applied to some types of patients and problems. To a lesser degree, this can also be said for biological models: The truth of their theory may be suspect, but treatment based on them is often effective.

Some have argued that the variability of theory and the failure of one to rise above all others suggest that "all have won and all must have prizes"—to quote from the well-known Lewis Carroll novel. We think that the most justified conclusion is threefold:

* Good therapists are good therapists, from whatever theoretical province they derive their skills. The power of these particular therapists is greater than any therapeutic contribution that may stem from any of these theories.
* Each theory constructs treatments that are beneficial for some but not all people. Thus, the most desirable course is to choose a therapist who can use the procedures from many theories, discriminately, depending on the patient and the problem.
* The fit between a patient's ideas about his or her problems and the therapist's explicit theory may be one of the most important ingredients in how successful a therapy will be.

In the next chapter, we will begin to explore the way a therapist's implicit and explicit theories come together in treatment. In the meantime, you may keep in mind two suggestions:

* It will be helpful if you are familiar with the explicit theories used by your therapist and their implications for treatment of your problems. If in the descriptions you have read here you find one that seems to fit your preferences as a way of being treated, then you should seek a therapist who expresses this type of viewpoint.
* Plan to ask any prospective therapist what they think causes personal problems and what is important in the successful treatment of your problems. You may even ask them to explain their theory of psychotherapy, applying it to your particular type of problem.

7

⌒

How We Discover
What Works

While therapists expect their patients to confuse their beliefs with reality, they are not as attentive to their own blind spots. Therapists are led by theories of behavior that they often take on faith. And like their patients, these private theories do affect their practices. An example might illustrate better how personal theories operate.

A number of years ago, one of us [LB] was sitting in his office at a small university in rural Texas when a young man approached and entered the office, asking, "Is this the place that has the machines?" He reported that somewhere in the building, there were machines, including a radio transmitter. He said the FBI was using the machines to broadcast thoughts to the inside of his head, and he was certain that he was being watched and that his life was in danger.

When asked to explain why the FBI would go to such efforts, he reported that he had received a visit from an angel who informed him that he was the reincarnation of Jesus Christ. The FBI, he said, was corrupt and was concerned that if he should ever come to power, they would be put out of business. He went on to explain that since being initially told of his own exalted position, the angel told him that he had until he was thirty-three years old to overcome these negative forces and bring down the corrupt government. Then, he said, God would insist he commit suicide.

As we have seen, a personal theory may sound reasonable if the initial assumptions can be believed. In this young man's case, if he can believe he is Jesus Christ, then the rest of his theory makes perfect sense. How do we prove he isn't who he says he is? In the 1950s, Milton Rokeach brought together three young psychiatric patients, all of whom shared two beliefs: that there was only one Jesus Christ, and that he was Jesus Christ. After three years of meeting together every day to discuss their common beliefs, only the first of these beliefs had changed. Each now believed that there were three Jesus Christs! Their second assumption remained unshaken.

If erroneous beliefs are to be changed, they must be checked against outside evidence. Even such personal beliefs as religion are stabilized and tested against external criteria such as established church doctrine or by reference to the Bible, the Tora, the Koran, or other religious documents. This chapter will explore the integration of science, the method of assessing and checking knowledge, and practice. We will describe both the role of science and the related attempts in clinical practice to apply treatment guidelines. In following chapters we will describe some of the experiences you might expect when you enter psychotherapy with a practitioner who attempts to use scientific principles to guide and develop that practice.

The Role of Science in Practice

While our theories, either implicit and personal or explicit and formal, cannot be proven, the effectiveness and value of our treatment strategies can be. We can look at what treatments work. What do we mean when we say something "works" or doesn't? In this chapter, we spell out whether there is scientific evidence that a particular theory works. If there is no proof, we will assume there is no reason to believe that a particular treatment does.

There are both advantages and disadvantages to accepting scientific criteria as evidence. For one thing, science has the disadvantage of being less stable than methods that do not require external validation and replication, such as religion, appeals to authority, or implicit theories based on personal experience. What is considered "true" by scientific criteria changes much easier and more rapidly than what is defined as "true" by appeals to authority, logic, or religion. Remember that science once asserted as "true" the concept that the sun, moon, and stars circled the Earth, or that bleeding a patient or using leeches was a sensible way of curing diseases.

Conclusions drawn from authorities or logic are resistant to change even when they are not accurate. Despite Galileo's physical evidence that the Earth circled the Sun, the church simply said it didn't and declared it heresy.

Modern science seldom talks about "facts" or "truths" in absolute terms. What is "true" and "factual" only can be seen through the knowledge and information available at a given time. As we learn more, truths and facts change. As we add new evidence to science, we modify or even overthrow former scientific truths. Not until Albert Einstein appeared were Isaac Newton's facts toppled.

In contrast, beliefs that don't rely on external evidence are governed by the strength of one's beliefs. Ordinarily, this means that they will remain stable even when evidence points to their being incorrect. This is called a closed system. It is closed because it does not let in any inconsistent information. A closed system protects old beliefs, keeping them stable by filtering new information and interpreting each new event in terms of an old belief. Religions, for example, may reject new information or accept it only insofar as doing so does not bring one into disagreement with his or her religion. New information is interpreted and assessed in ways that do not shake the basis of faith in the defined truths. When "truths" or prophecies based on strong belief, such as religion, private and implicit theory, or the power of authority, fail to predict as they promise, the predictions can be revised without jeopardizing the belief or "truth." Think of all the "prophets" who predicted the end of the world at specific dates. When those dates passed, the prophets could claim that "God changed his mind" or "Fallible disciples misinterpreted the master's authority."

The scientific method, however, specifically allows the results of truth-gathering efforts to change the nature of the thing originally called "truth." The scientific method is based on the assumption that only when "truth" can change to accommodate new information will we advance as a community of people. So, through the scientific method, doctors stopped bleeding patients. Likewise, science overthrew the beliefs that humans could not fly, that demons caused disease, and that God's anger caused fire—all accepted truths at one time. Left only to religious or other implicit belief systems, these views of the world would never have changed. Even now, some religions argue that the world is flat or square, based on the biblical comment about there being four corners of the earth.

En route to an enduring truth, the person who elects to put faith in scientific evidence must suffer through contradictions. He or she must have a high tolerance for change and ambiguity. The good news is that the methods of science have served us well in advancing our knowledge and achievements. It is, arguably, the most direct way to ascertaining the nature of the world. To assess the effectiveness of health and mental health care, it is the only viable way that we know to obtain factual and reliable information.

But we must not overrate science as a method of obtaining access to knowledge. It is fallible, inexact, probabilistic, and often frustrating. Its truths often are punctuated by false starts and misdirection. Not unlike other methods of defining truth, one who selects science as the basis for knowledge does so through a leap of faith. There are many holes in the fabric of knowledge still unfilled.

At some level, it comes down to making our choices about what methods we will accept to ascertain what "truth" is. Will it be an act of informed (as opposed to blind) faith, or will it be the knee-jerk, usual response of deciding truth by what keeps one comfortable and free from distress? We know a great deal about the attributes of therapists and patients that correlate with treatment success. We know a little about what treatments are effective in producing changes. We know a bit about which are more or less effective. But we don't yet know whether most forms of treatment work or not. On the other hand, relying solely on scientific knowledge, it is difficult to attribute the destructive effects of treatment to specific procedures of psychotherapy. Yet, science still holds the promise of helping us determine what things actually help and which do not. That is an advantage that counterbalances the legal and professional rules and procedures that, as we've seen, can only identify dangerous and unprofessional practices.

The Need for and Nature of Treatment Guidelines

In an uncertain world, psychotherapists often construct their own sets of "facts," not based on scientific evidence, but on their own beliefs, personal experiences, hunches, and philosophies. We occasionally hear how the intuition of a scientist led to great advances of knowledge, but this is the exception, not the rule. A scientist's beliefs are often wrong. Sometimes, despite their best efforts and good intentions, they construct facts to carry them through the dilemma of uncertainty, only to be later proven wrong. But error in science sometimes advances the field almost as much as being right.

There is a place for faith in professional practice, but it is a faith in people, not in theories, that is justified.

As applied to psychotherapy, scientific research now tells us, and it is fortunate, that usually the skill and nonspecific interventions of the therapist outweigh the use of ineffective and even destructive procedures that arise from good intentions and strongly held beliefs. The skill of the therapist is a much more powerful determiner of benefit than the nature of the procedures themselves. Hence, even poor techniques in the hands of good therapists will often produce good effects. Many patients who are looking for help are simply demoralized. Jerome Frank, of Johns Hopkins University, once observed that the role of a good mental health practitioner is to "remoralize." The value of hope, as a catalyst of therapy, is well known and well documented.

Of course, the converse also is true; even powerful techniques in the hands of a poor therapist can produce poor effects. Nonetheless, it is an unavoidable conclusion that some procedures are more likely than others to produce benefit, depending on the nature of the patient and the problem, and that the use of certain procedures is particularly risky, no matter who uses them. Some have a lower than average likelihood of paying off, while others have a higher than average chance of exerting positive effects.

We can establish the effectiveness of psychotherapy only by systematic scientific investigations. Before describing what works for different types of problems (Chapter 8), we must revisit the question raised in Chapter 1 about how one decides when something is true. This time, we will address our considerations to how science and scientists define and identify what treatments are effective and which are not.

There is no single or uniform criterion that science uses to define "truth." Truth is always probabilistic, and heated debates rage among scientists about what type of evidence and how many replications of findings are required before something can be considered factual. The answers to these questions vary as a function of how science is carried out.

Moreover, even within a field, there may be intense arguments about whether the available evidence is sufficient to allow a general conclusion of fact. Each discipline of science establishes criteria that define an acceptable rate of error in interpreting a particular research study. Usually, in science, a given scientific finding in a single experimental study is considered accurate if there is less than a 5 percent chance that it could have occurred by random chance or bias of the methods. Scientists use mathematical formulas and calculations, based on both observations and theories of probability, to estimate these error rates for each finding. Frequently, one study will demonstrate one finding and another will show the opposite, both at the same level of confidence in the findings. This is expected in a probabilistic world and is why we find it somewhat amusing when someone suggests once again that still another something we eat is linked to cancer. Acceptance of such "facts" depends on replication.

Scientists are thus faced with the question of how many demonstrations of a finding are necessary before one can begin using the new knowledge to provide treatment. For this, there are no established standards. The Federal Drug Administration requires at least two demonstrations from different controlled and blind studies that a given drug produces a positive effect. Each study must be able to draw that conclusion with less than a 5 percent chance of error. Frequently, if the drug has been widely researched, there may be many other studies that failed to find any effect at all; if the drug is new, only those two studies may be available.

In recent years, the professions of clinical psychology and psychiatry have begun to develop and write explicit guidelines for treating different types of problems and patients. Publishing treatment guidelines is a way of summarizing often contradictory findings across many studies to offer the practitioner the best information available from science about how to practice.

Guidelines, for the more part, arise from two somewhat overlapping processes. They either represent a set of consensual statements from major figures in the field regarding what they think are the essential ingredients of an effective treatment—consensus panels— or they are a summary derived directly from empirical evidence of what constitutes effective treatment.

A Quick Course in Research Design

Suppose you have a cold. Your doctor gives you a potion and you get better about a week later. Did the treatment work?

You may think it did and be satisfied with the treatment. Since colds usually go away by themselves in seven to ten days, the only way we can determine if the treatment worked is to compare your response to patients with the same or similar symptoms who did not receive treatment. Whether the patient attributes the cure to the medication or not is immaterial from a standard of scientific evidence, since these attributions are fallible.

In mental health, the scientist is interested in finding out if a given treatment produces an effect that is significantly greater than if the therapist simply sat there and listened to you, or even if the therapist never showed up. Remember that 14 percent of people get better just by making an appointment with the therapist.

It may seem easy enough to simply give the treatment and then observe the change that follows. This is the approach used by clinicians and is the basis for their drawing conclusions based on "clinical experience."

For example, in a study of adult women who had suffered problems after being molested as children, researchers tried to see if group therapy helped. They organized five therapy groups with a total of twenty-eight women. The groups met once a week for ten weeks with the methods used in each group planned in advance and monitored to ensure that all treatments were similar. They observed that, both at the end of treatment and six months later, most women reported that the group had been helpful.

First, this research seems to offer some important conclusions about the effectiveness of group therapy. However, the methods used to study group therapy in this study have some decided limitations, and without knowing these, the findings might seduce the observer into reaching a premature conclusion that group treatment causes people to feel better.

Patient satisfaction is not the same as improvement. Often patients who feel hopeless about their conditions are satisfied by the therapist's care and support even though they do not get better. In other instances, people get better just because someone pays attention to them. In physical medicine, we call this the placebo effect, the well-documented phenomenon that a predictable number of patients who received sugar pills still get better. The expression of caring invokes change. People expect to be helped and so they feel better.

Treatments must demonstrate that they are truly effective— that they produce some lasting change in the patient's problems— not just satisfaction.

Second, even if benefits occur, improvement felt at the end of group therapy might be the result of many things that had nothing to do with the treatment itself. Many feelings of emotional distress, for example, improve spontaneously. These conditions might change without any treatment at all. Other conditions and levels of distress change as long as some minimal amount of support and help are available, regardless of the form. And sometimes peoples' lives change because of unpredictable external variables that have nothing to do with treatment, such as falling in love or winning the lottery.

It is likely that at least some of the patients who were satisfied at the end of group therapy benefited because of "nonspecific" factors that would be a part of any treatment, not just group treatment sessions: natural changes in the condition or symptom, the support and caring nature of the therapist, and so on.

From whatever cause, people may misattribute such changes to the group, since that is what they were doing at the time the improvement occurred. But since many factors often influence our lives at once, scientists are also interested in what they call "treatment mediators." Mediators are those things that may facilitate or inhibit the effects of treatment. A treatment may work if a person possesses certain mediators but does not work if these factors are missing or are at a different level. For example, the scientist may want to know if the level of patient anxiety or the availability of social support from family members increases or decreases the likelihood or the magnitude of the effects produced by a given treatment.

The question, does C follow A, is simplistic. What we really want to know is not whether improvement follows treatment, but

- If the treatment can produce an improvement faster than can be expected to occur without treatment?
- If the treatment enhances the effectiveness of a particular therapist.
- Is the treatment more effective than just having the therapist care for and support the patient?
- If the improvement will be maintained better than receiving no treatment or a nonspecific treatment alone?
- If the treatment will work among those for whom improvement would not ordinarily be expected?
- If there are characteristics of the patient that make them more responsive to some treatments and less responsive to others?

It is not enough to show that the condition or problem got better following treatment. We have to be able to conclude with some confidence that it changes BECAUSE of the specific procedures used in that treatment. Research usually looks at average responses among groups of individuals who are either randomly assigned (like drawing lots) to receive or not receive the treatment, or who are matched to one another in some way. If the treated group has a higher average response than either an untreated group or a group that gets a placebo treatment, then one may conclude that the treatment works either to increase rate, magnitude, or retention of the response.

However, scientific findings are not absolute. There is a scientific fiction in the notion that if twelve monkeys were turned loose in a room full of typewriters, one would eventually produce *Hamlet*. The probability of this complex activity occurring by random chance is so small that, if in fact the monkeys managed to produce the text, the most logical conclusion would be to assume that, the monkeys had learned to write rather than that the works were produced entirely by chance.

Hence, scientists use mathematically based procedures (statistics) to estimate the likelihood of an observation occurring by chance. Considering what we know of how various characteristics, outcomes, and other variables are distributed among people, scientific findings can be presented in terms of probabilities.

But accepting the standard 5 percent rule mentioned earlier has a downside: Any scientific finding, no matter how carefully designed and important the study, still has about a 5 percent chance of being wrong. More poorly designed studies may have an even higher probability. Each subsequent, confirming finding decreases the probability of error. The link between lung cancer and tobacco use was not based on a single study, but on years of similar results from different studies, with no single one conclusively proving causation.

While scientists understand this, the media frequently base conclusions on single studies and findings. Be wary of placing confidence in reports from the mass media that cite only one study. Researchers wait for findings to accumulate across time and populations. And as studies accumulate, researchers and laypeople alike can begin to place more faith in the findings. Still, the results only describe a probability that the treatment is effective. Any final conclusions about what types of procedures work and which don't must take into account the type of research design.

The *randomized clinical trial* design is often considered the gold standard of scientific testing. In this method, researchers select a carefully defined and measured sample of patients. These subjects are randomly assigned to either the treatment or control groups (people who don't get the treatment) to minimize the likelihood of bias. Treatments are provided in ways that ensure that both groups are treated in the same way, except in the treatment being tested. Patients are all recruited in the same way, the explanations given to them about the study are the same, the assessment and measures used are the same, even the treatments are of similar length and intensity.

Then outcomes are assessed and evaluated independently of either the doctor's bias or the patient's memory. Even the scientists don't know which group gets what—the reason the tests are called "blind."

By keeping the scientist "blind" you control for the scientist's expectancies and preferences of treatment. The amount of time spent and the amount of conversation and attention given to the patient will be carefully controlled by scripting the precise activities of those administering the treatment. These activities will be monitored to make sure that the clinician complies with the script. This will guarantee that all patients get similar treatment and that the doctors' levels of caring and interest are the same in the two treatment conditions.

However, to see if the findings from such studies can be generalized into usual practices and usual patients, a different kind of study is required. Research on effectiveness studies fills this need. Effectiveness studies evaluate treatments in their usual settings over long periods of time, and rather than applying the treatment only to select cases of highly screened patients, they study the patients who usually and typically have the problems in question. It remains, however, that the randomized study provides the clearest definition of the components of treatment and the clearest evidence of treatment efficacy.

These are the kinds of tests we will review as we analyze which treatments work and which do not in Chapter 8.

Beginning Effective Treatment: What to Expect

Research tells us what is effective, it informs us of the importance of the treatment relationship, the role played by the patient's and therapist's expectations, the effect of hope and positive attitudes, and the role of trust and caring. Now it is time that we blend this research perspective with what actually happens in practice. In this section, we will review what you might expect in a typical therapy session as the therapist attempts both to gather important information by which to plan your treatment and begins to develop a working relationship with you. This will afford us an opportunity to address some of the problems that result when we blend science with practice.

During the first few sessions you attend in a clinic or therapist's office, the focus will be on evaluating the nature of your problem. Ostensibly, this will help the therapist determine what treatment you will be offered. If one doesn't rely on scientific findings and procedures, it is likely that the better predictor of which treatment you will be offered is the treatment that was offered to the last person who came through the door. Treatment decisions, often, are not as well governed by guidelines and evidence as one might hope, but, to the degree that they are, you can expect that the therapist will attempt to gather a lot of information and will talk to you about what this information means in terms of your treatment. If it is not clear, you should ask questions and discuss your problem with the therapist, making sure you understand the nature of the treatment—and agree with it.

Usually the person who will serve as your therapist will conduct the initial evaluation, but not always. Research suggests that having the same person conduct the evaluation and the treatment is more satisfying and less frustrating to patients than having someone else do it, but you cannot count on this in a busy clinic. In either case, at some time in this process most therapists will conduct what is called a "mental status examination," which includes an interview and a set of structured tasks that involve computation, memory, drawing, and word games.

Rather than doing these structured tasks as part of the interview, other therapists obtain some of this information by asking you to fill out several paper-and-pencil questionnaires. There are advantages to this latter procedure, though it is infrequently done. It is an efficient and reliable way for the therapist to obtain information about your personality, symptoms, and social functioning. These tests can be time consuming, but may substantially decrease the amount of professional time needed and reduce your cost in the long run if they are used to make distinctive treatment decisions. Tests have the advantage over interview-based procedures in providing scientifically defined standards against which to assess the nature and seriousness of your problem. If used correctly, these tests can not only supply important information about the nature of your problem, but can suggest the type of treatment that may be most helpful.

Research tells us that these formal tests provide more valid and reliable data than the usual mental status examination and interview, but therapists have such (ill-founded) faith in their own judgments that most don't use such tests. Patients also like the personal contact of the individual interview better than filling out forms. Instead of excluding the most valid procedures in favor of the most comfortable, we recommend both formal tests and interviews.

By whatever procedure, the central goal of the initial evaluation is to obtain information about the problems that have brought you to treatment. This information will probably include:

- A history of the problem—when it started, how consistent or persistent it is, and the effects of prior treatment efforts.
- A description of the symptoms—the level to which they interfere with your day-to-day activities, including going to work or school, or ability to plan and concentrate. Depression and anxiety, for example, may make it difficult for you to focus your attention and may even interfere with your ability to remember important appointments and activities. Your activities may become disorganized and even your thoughts may get confused and interfere with your ability to be understood.
- Family history—background on your family, marriages, and significant early experiences.
- Social history—a review of social relationships and problems, including level of education, legal problems, recreational drug and alcohol use, recurrent problems in intimate, marriage-like relationships, and availability of friendships.
- Medical history—an inquiry about medical problems, including accidents, illnesses, treatments, reactions to medications, residual symptoms, and continuing treatments.

In the process of reviewing these various histories, the therapist will try to find out how well you are able to think through problems, assess options, and remain open to alternative solutions. This will probably entail asking questions about your memory, any unusual experiences you've had, and questions about whether you have ever experienced hallucinations, out-of-body experiences, or feelings that things around you were not real.

Most research indicates that it is important to get specific information on sexual functioning and attitudes, religious beliefs and background, and evidence of early sexual, physical, or emotional abuse. These topics are often ignored by therapists in the first few interviews, however. If the interviewer doesn't ask these questions, it may mean that she simply hasn't yet had the time to bring them up, or it could mean that she is uncomfortable with these topics. If you sense your therapist is uncomfortable discussing these matters, you should be concerned that this person may have difficulty helping you with problems that involve such sensitive subjects. If you have concerns about emotional or sexual subjects, it is important that you too feel comfortable discussing these things. Do your own assessment of whether they are topics that are difficult for the therapist to discuss with you. If you sense a problem and cannot bring it up, you may want to consider a different therapist.

As you review differences in research guidelines and the conventional procedures of practice, remember two things:

- *Research tells us that therapists not therapies are the most important contributors to effectiveness.* Certain therapists have relatively strong and positive effects, while others have nearly as consistent negative effects. Most good treatment outcomes are produced against a background of fundamental trust in a therapist who is confident, kind, and understanding.
- *Guidelines are not rules.* There are always situations in which an empirically tested treatment is not likely to be effective and another option may be justified. If the structure of treatment you are receiving does not reflect the guidelines described here, you should raise questions, especially if you are not making satisfactory progress.

With more than 400 different types of treatment, you may wonder how we can summarize the effective ones in just a few pages. Unfortunately, *by far the majority of therapies have yet to receive the barest thread of evidence of having specific effects beyond those expected from a caring and supportive therapist who merely listens and observes.*

That cuts our work load considerably.

The Task Force on Promotion and Dissemination of Psychological

Procedures, set up by the American Psychological Association, identified only eighteen specific treatments whose effectiveness they considered to have been established for psychotherapy. These fell into six basic treatment groups that parallel the ones we have already reviewed in Chapter 6. Updated reports have added a number of other treatments and included several specific suggestions about matching certain treatments to patients with personality dimensions other than those used for making diagnostic decisions.

The remaining 300+ treatments continue in wide practice, not because we know they work but because we have not produced convincing evidence that they don't.

So, how do you pick a therapist? What treatment is effective for your problem?

In the next chapter, we'll tell you.

GUIDELINES TO KEEP IN MIND

A well-meaning therapist can legally practice almost any type of treatment that seems logical—there is no law that says you must be offered an effective treatment. However, a mental health practitioner has a moral and ethical obligation to provide you with the best treatment available. The best evidence of what is the best treatment, we believe, arises from scientific findings.

Science and scientific evidence offer the optimal and surest access to helping the therapist avoid violating the boundary between personal beliefs and professional practices. We encourage you to ask your therapist the scientific evidence for the type of treatment that you are receiving.

Specifically, we offer the following suggestions and recommendations:

* Be alert to signs that the therapist has an undue investment in convincing you of her viewpoint, suggestions, and interpretations that you don't agree with or that seem a little far-fetched. Especially be concerned if your therapist relies on the unsubstantiated opinions of experts to convince you of a point of view.

* Seek information about external evidence and research that confirms or rejects the points of view with which you don't agree.
* Ask your therapist to describe his general approach and recommendations.
* Try to imagine, discover, and discuss alternative explanations to those offered by the therapist for your problems. Be willing to consider all possibilities that seem reasonable.
* Don't shy away from seeking a second opinion if your therapist engages in practices that do not seem helpful or ones you disagree with. Preferably, do this after discussing these practices with your therapist.

To help you, in the next chapter we will offer some general descriptions of what to expect and the treatment procedures whose use is most supportable on scientific grounds. As time passes, the list of empirically validated treatments will change, as it should, but we offer a brief outline of what treatments we think the best evidence will support.

8

⁓

What Works with
What Problems?

We now turn our attention to the actual procedures you will encounter in the therapist's office once treatment begins. Here, we outline some of the major treatments, particularly psychotherapies, found to be helpful for the treatment of different problems—depression, anxiety, various phobias, and so forth.

Obviously, neither our lists of problems nor treatments are exhaustive, but we have picked and described those treatments that have been adopted as guidelines by consensus panels and scientific summaries for meeting at least the minimal criteria of having generated a body of supportive scientific research. We repeat: The absence of a particular approach in our listing should not be of concern if you think your treatment is progressing satisfactorily. But, if your treatment is not proceeding well, the treatments described here might enable you to initiate a conversation with your therapist about changing the nature of your treatment.

We intend our recommendations to facilitate your dialogue with your clinician. We do not mean them to be used as the basis for threat, accusation, or claims of ethical and legal violations. To be a good patient—one who contributes to your own treatment—you need to be informed, and information should come from your therapist first. Our descriptions are designed, first, to help you see how your therapist may view your problem and, second, to help you identify when you are getting treatments that have been well established as effective by scientific test.

The descriptions that we will provide of treatments are not intended to be exhaustive, but they can serve as standards against which you can compare the treatment(s) you are receiving.

Because of the bias and untrustworthiness of subjective judgments, we have adopted the standard that an adequate demonstration of a treatment's effectiveness includes at least two controlled experimental tests in which the treatment is compared to those who receive no treatment, an established alternative treatment, or a placebo treatment.

At the end of this chapter, we provide a quick-reference chart that summarizes our findings.

Depression

Most people think they can recognize when they are depressed. But mental health professionals think of depression as a spectrum of disorders, each with a variety of symptoms, and only one of those symptoms may be a depressed mood. Theoretically, you may be diagnosed as having a depressive spectrum disorder and not be aware that you are unhappy. This seems like a contradiction, but two factors may account for this disparity.

First, you may have been depressed all of your life and have become used to it. This may distort your picture of what is normal or usual. You may only assess your own internal state against your usual state to decide if something is wrong. If you've always been depressed, but what you experience now is not unusual, then you may be unaware of being unhappy.

Second, the diagnosis of depression itself may be a problem. Research has not been able to establish that depression, with the possible exception of what has been variously called bipolar disorder and manic depressive disorder, can be identified and distinguished from other conditions such as anxiety. Symptoms of depression occur in many varieties and within the context of many different problems. Clinically, we think of syndromes like depression as collections of symptoms that seem to aggregate together. Whether this is true, it is possible that some symptoms will be present and others won't. One can qualify as having one of the depressive spectrum disorders, such as major depressive disorder, by the presence only of some symptoms, for example. Unhappiness may not be among them.

What symptoms are manifest in your life are a function of how long and how severe your problems are. Consensus panels and treatment guidelines conclude that if you seem depressed, you should be asked to provide specific information about the type and nature of past losses. These may include deaths of family members, abandonment by significant others, lost jobs, and so on. If you have experienced a number of such events, the therapist should review with you any suicidal thoughts and patterns in their appearance, past or present suicidal behavior or plans, and a description of your symptoms.

Biological Views

If your therapist or doctor adopts a biological model of behavior to guide her treatment, she may look for the presence of some symptoms (vegetative signs—disturbances in appetite, sexual desires, social pleasure, energy, sleep patterns, and quality of work and interpersonal activities) as an indicator for whether to use medication. If you have several of these signs, it is likely that your therapist will prescribe antidepressant medications.

If your therapist is a psychiatrist, with a medical degree, it is more likely that she will adopt a biological view of your behavior. The presence of these signs will be taken by her to indicate that the depression is "biological" and results from a "chemical imbalance." While it may be helpful for you to receive antidepressant medication, psychotherapeutically based treatments may still be of benefit to you as well.

In fact, science has not yet revealed if biological factors and the symptoms they initiate follow from your depressed state or whether they cause your feelings. It seems clear that medications do help reduce the intensity of debilitating vegetative patterns. The usual medications will be either Prozac, one of its equivalents, or one of several TCAs (tricyclic antidepressants), such as Elavil.

Research suggests that while medication and psychotherapy are equally effective in the short run, drugs seem to work faster, and psychotherapy seems to last longer.

You should also keep in mind that while medication will have its strongest effects on the vegetative signs themselves, psychotherapy exerts more impact on life functioning and social impairment. Given that these different therapies cover different features of your disorder, some consensus panels have recommended the combination of medication and psychotherapy. While this seems logical, it is not entirely supportable from empirical research, except possibly for some of the more serious forms of depression. Not only are many people intolerant of one or the other form of therapy, but a substantial body of research indicates that for most depressive states, the combined effects of drugs and medication over the long run provide no better effects than psychotherapy alone. This may be particularly true for some types of psychotherapy, a point we will cover shortly.

Psychotherapy

Besides biological models, which support the use of antidepressant medications, available research provides reasonably good support for the use and value of two variations of psychotherapy derived from *behavioral-cognitive traditions* and one from *interpersonal-systems* approaches. A model of psychodynamic therapy has received more limited but promising support as being effective, and we will review this as well.

Psychotherapy is an effective treatment for most depression, though it is thought to be least appropriate as the sole treatment for bipolar disorder. In treatments for non-bipolar depression, research tells us that you can expect to begin experiencing some initial, but often unstable, positive changes by the tenth or twelfth week of treatment. Usually it takes this long for symptoms to begin to change, but you might notice a sense of increased optimism and hope before this time. Some people take longer than others, however, and a return to normal functioning is highly dependent on the complexity of the problem.

If you are considering psychotherapy, approximately half of those who seek treatment for depression experience a noticeable relief of symptoms after about three months—that is, about twenty-five weekly psychotherapy sessions. Eighty percent of depressed people return to near normal functioning and feel well by the end of a year of treatment. But there is still some controversy over the likelihood of relapse after psychotherapy. Some summaries have indicated that relapse rates are surprisingly low, while others suggest that nearly two-thirds of people will have another episode of depression within a year. Apparently, those who have had at least two prior episodes of similar symptoms and problems are at risk of relapse and should protect themselves with ongoing, even if periodic, treatment. Effective treatment reduces but does not completely eliminate recurrence, but it does seem to make these relapses somewhat shorter for most people.

Those who have the longest histories of depression, especially people who cannot remember a period of more than a few months when they were not depressed during their adult lives, may ultimately have to reconcile themselves to periodic and recurrent treatment for an extended time.

COGNITIVE MODELS

Cognitive therapy is a method of intervening directly with the behavioral symptoms of depression through the medium of looking at and altering how one thinks about one's problems. For people suffering from depression, cognitive therapy is effectively dispensed within about twenty sessions. This time frame ordinarily results in some change of symptoms and improved outlook. The treatment is appropriate for treating major, single-episode or recurring depression.

You cannot count on treatment for depression in any model to be short term. Symptoms of depression are recurrent, complex, and multidimensional, and treatment can take some fine-tuning—and time—regardless of what model of behavior serves as the foundation for the intervention. Some treatments based on a cognitive model are quite long, particularly for those patients who display suicidal tendencies or those with unstable life circumstances.

Several cognitive models of therapy are available to treat depression and associated symptoms such as suicidal behaviors. These models all assume that depression results from:

- Inconsistent attributions of events—bad events are seen as personally caused; positive events are the result of luck or other people
- Inaccurate appraisals—bad things happen frequently, good things rarely
- Dysfunctional information processing—selective attention
- The presence of self-critical internal voices

Cognitive models assume that people can avoid being trapped in depression by these thoughts if they learn to reappraise and correct them. The therapist who adopts one of the available cognitive models is partially a teacher and partially a collaborator. In this role, he will question you about the nature of your thoughts and why you think you are depressed.

He will take time to instruct and explain how thoughts and beliefs, not situations, cause depression. You will have homework assignments, as well as other procedures that structure and control the course of treatment. You may be put on an explicit contract to attend sessions and complete the homework assignments.

Early in treatment, these homework assignments may take the form of reading and trying to become more active in social activities. You may be given a workbook to help you learn the concepts that are being taught. If you have many suicidal impulses and thoughts, you may be asked to monitor and record them, and promise to avoid trying to kill yourself. As therapy progresses beyond the first few sessions, you will probably keep records of other thoughts and feelings, along with the situations in which they occur. In this process, you will be taught to identify what thoughts are dysfunctional or inaccurate and to begin a process of logical criticism.

By using the records and self-observations generated in homework assignments, the therapist hopes that you will learn and then accept the philosophy that beliefs, not situations, cause problems. The therapist wants you to learn the nature of the disruptions and distortions that occur in your thought processes when bad things happen, and then to identify and practice new ways of interpreting these events. Later in treatment, these assignments will concentrate on replacing habitual ways of thinking and behaving with new thoughts and behaviors to increase levels of pleasure and social support.

The therapist who uses cognitive therapy tends to rely on questions, teaching, and structured homework assignments. The importance of personal discovery is emphasized, but this does not mean reviewing your early experience. It means that you will adopt an attitude of exploration about your problems and discover ways to identify inaccurate and destructive beliefs, challenge these thoughts and beliefs, and develop methods of replacing these faulty beliefs with more accurate and rational alternatives.

A variety of procedures have been developed specifically to address the critical and second-person ("You will never make anything of yourself") character of many negative thoughts, particularly those of a suicidal and destructive nature. One such procedure entails learning to identify and express aloud the critical and hostile thought pattern, first in the usual second-person voice and then in different forms. This allows an inspection of the inner voice: it is followed by a process of learning to talk back to, and even replace, the content of these "inner voices" with more positive qualities.

Cognitive therapy represents the clearest example of a therapy that does not consistently combine well with medication. Several well-designed studies indicate that medication produces effects somewhat faster than those from cognitive therapy, but when medication and cognitive therapy are combined, the amount of improvement is sometimes less than when either is used alone. After about twenty sessions, when antidepressant medication is compared to cognitive therapy, among non-bipolar patients, the results are equivalent.

Cognitive therapy does not work equally well with all depressed individuals. Because it is most concerned with the external expression of thought processes, it appears to do best in people who are expressive and active—those whose general approach to life is external, who enjoy social activities, and whom others see as impulsive and troublesome because of their behavior. It works least well among those who are especially self-critical, who become indecisive, who tend to withdraw and brood about their problems, and who have never particularly enjoyed social gatherings—those internally focused.

Because cognitive therapy is also therapist guided, it seems to do poorly with patients whom others judge to be stubborn, defensive, resistant to being guided, oppositional, or negative. Those who have trouble taking directions from others and frequently get into arguments defending their beliefs and opinions are prone to do somewhat worse than those who are more passive and accepting of direction. If you hate taking direction, you will not acclimate well to the teacher-like stance of the therapist.

Unfortunately, sometimes a person is not the best judge of whether he or she is one of these "defensive" people. This judgment seems best obtained by asking how other people see you. If you have a hard time soliciting, hearing, or accepting their feedback, it may be a good sign that you are a bit defensive. Although cognitive therapy remains an option, you are likely to find other, less therapist-guided approaches (e.g., humanistic therapy, systems therapy, and psychoanalytic models) somewhat more compatible.

BEHAVIORAL APPROACH

Social skills training is a second effective treatment based on a behavioral model of intervention. Even more than cognitive therapy, the focus of social skills training is on overt rather than internal behavior, and on the role of consequences in altering and maintaining depression. This treatment has been found to be particularly helpful for patients who lack the ability to develop and maintain relationships with other people, as indicated by their recurrent difficulties with intimate, social, family, and work relationships.

Social skills training attempts to teach patients to achieve meaningful relationships by learning to communicate clearly with others, accurately evaluate themselves, and reward themselves for successes.

During and after evaluating your problems, the therapist who follows this model relies on direct instruction, demonstration, role-playing, coaching, and practice both within the session and afterward. The rationale for the approach will be explained to you, as will a summary of the nature of the procedures employed to ensure learning the new skills needed to treat your depression. The skills identi-

fied, described, and practiced in the therapy session are then reinforced in practice sessions.

The therapist typically will demonstrate some of the skills you
must learn, and then conduct a practice session. Response, discussion, and more practice follow. At each step, you should expect to
receive feedback, praise for success, and other rewards that might
enhance your learning.

Performance sessions continue until identified skills are "over-
trained"—practiced in their acceptable form several times. As a last
step, you will learn to evaluate yourself and reward yourself for
good behavior.

The creators of this model of treatment are straightforward in
pointing out that while this treatment works for many, it does not
work for all depressed patients. It may be best for those who have
specific problems in expressing praise or criticizing others. The more
complex the problem and the more broad-ranging and severe the
symptoms, the less effective this type of intervention is likely to be.

INTERPERSONAL PSYCHOTHERAPY

Interpersonal psychotherapy or IPT, a time-limited (sixteen to twenty sessions) therapy, is a variation of the systems-interpersonal models and with depression is applied to one or two interpersonal
problem areas related to the patient's complaints. The focus of IPT
is on current social relationships, although some brief discussion of
past relationships is sometimes useful in clarifying the nature of patterns that might influence current ones.

The strategies of IPT differ somewhat across three phases of treatment. The first few sessions are committed to diagnosing the nature
of your depression and giving you a rationale for the symptoms that
are present. Unlike the reasoning given in cognitive therapy, this
rationale is framed in medical terms, thus introducing some aspects
of a biological model of behavior into the treatment.

You will be told that your depression is a medical problem and
should be treated that way, by following the advice of your doctor and
allowing yourself time to get over it. The therapist also will explain
the natural, cyclical course of depression, describe the symptoms that
usually accompany depression, and help you anticipate where you are

in the cycle. This type of therapy is often combined with antidepressant medications and seems to benefit from this combination.

The therapist's stance varies from being passively reflective to directive and educational, depending on the nature of the problem or problems assumed to underlie the depression. IPT is a varied and flexible approach, one that can be quite useful if the idea that you have a "biological depression" or that your behavior is an "illness" appeals to you. Many people gravitate to this view, while others find it unhelpful.

Research suggests that interpersonal models work best among patients who have clearly identifiable interpersonal problems and who value relationships with other people very highly. These patients tend to be socially sensitive, somewhat insecure, and uncertain of themselves in social groups. They worry too much about how others perceive them and inhibit their impulses, dissatisfaction, and emotions to protect others' feelings. To work well in this treatment, of course, you must accept being directed and guided by your therapist's expertise.

Again, the length of therapy may be somewhat longer than usual if the problem is particularly complex.

PSYCHODYNAMIC APPROACH

Psychodynamic therapy has also been found to be at least modestly successful in reducing depression. The characteristics of those interventions found to be effective in treating depression include the establishment of time limits to define how long treatment will last and the identification of a very focused theme or pattern that characterizes an individual's relationships with other people. This treatment ordinarily is limited to fewer than forty sessions—relatively short for psychodynamic models of treatment—and seeks to identify and then understand the motives that result in recurrent interpersonal difficulties.

The therapist working from this model will ask you to review important relationships until you can identify a recurrent, core conflict and response pattern that characterizes these relationships. While the nature of how the therapist conceptualizes these themes may differ somewhat, most identify a consistent set of needs and goals (need for love, nurturance, independence, recognition, and so on) that lead to the initiation of the relationship, and the countering effects of fears and apprehensions (fear of rejection, fear of punishment, fear of criticism, and so on) that produce conflict and undermine the realization of goals.

Sessions will be devoted to helping you recognize these patterns, including their manifestation in your interactions with the therapist and to understanding the nature of the needs and conflicts represented in them. The therapist, while not passive, will exert less control on the treatment than is true of the other therapies described here.

Psychodynamic interventions begin with a relatively lengthy evaluation period—three or more sessions. In these sessions, your history of relationships and past depressions are explored in depth. From this, the therapist develops and presents to you a picture or formulation of the problem. These formulations differ from one psychodynamic model of therapy or from one therapist to another, but they are consistent in that they identify the major wants or conflicts that characterize your most important relationships. The therapist will identify different expectations that you might have about attempting to express your wishes or impulses.

The symptoms of depression are thought to reflect a compromise between your wishes and your fears. They represent efforts to protect yourself in the face of this conflict. Thus, your symptoms serve as the basis for analyzing your motives, the relationship with your therapist, and the nature of your depression.

Treatment from a psychodynamic model relies heavily on the therapist providing a believable and acceptable interpretation of why and how you developed various wishes and impulses, and an explanation of the conflicts that develop from them. This means undergoing an assessment of your early development, relationships with your parents and siblings and transferring the insights gathered to an understanding of why you are depressed in your present relationships.

It is not yet clear for whom psychodynamic models are most and least effective. Some research suggests that individuals least likely to do well in cognitive therapy—those who are self-reflective, uncomfortable with rules, introverted—may be the people most likely to do well with psychodynamic therapies. If this description fits you and if you have had repeated problems initiating or maintaining close relationships, a pattern that seems to be associated with your periods of depression, then it may be worth your while to seek out a therapist who uses a time-limited, psychodynamic therapy.

Anxiety

Like depression, anxiety is a condition we are all familiar with in some form or another and to some degree or another. We all have it and might occasionally benefit from some help with controlling it. The symptoms of anxiety become a "disorder" when they are persistent and interrupt normal life.

Anxiety and depression are difficult to distinguish. You feel unhappy, indecisive, have trouble sleeping, and feel general distress in both cases. They may both be associated with vague and often difficult-to-diagnose physical complaints such as headaches and stomachaches, or aches and pains in the joints not related to other medical disorders. Because of these similarities of feelings, clinicians distinguish anxiety from depression more from the overt symptoms than from the subjective ones. When overt symptoms of anxiety (e.g., phobias, sleep disturbances, and so on) occur and interrupt your life, you have developed an anxiety disorder.

Treatments for anxiety disorders focus on one or more of three areas: (1) the evoking events in the environment that initiate the anxiety, (2) the symptoms of anxiety and dysfunction themselves, or (3) the resulting avoidance behaviors that are designed to reduce the anxiety. Evoking events may include remembrances of past anxiety events as well as those in the external world. These treatments use procedures to expose the patient to the provoking events while preventing withdrawal and avoidance. This is a process of extinction.

Symptoms may also be addressed directly by reinforcing change and establishing a behavioral repertoire that is incompatible with the manifestation of these symptoms. One may learn to relax in anxiety situations, for example. Since relaxation and tension are incompatible, the relaxation response can replace the anxiety response.

Prevention of avoidance also encourages extinction by holding the patient in the frightening environment. This procedure usually comes with making changes in the provoking, environmental events.

Although depression is a very general condition (nearly 40 percent of those who have an anxiety disorder are also depressed), anxiety is more specific and differentiated. There are other differences as well. While depression typically passes over a period of weeks, symptoms of anxiety are less likely to go away on their own. Once established, they don't disappear without treatment. Clearly, depression accompanies anxiety for many people, but a much smaller percentage of people with depression also develop symptoms of anxiety that impair them. While many people who have depression can get by without treatment so long as they become used to and learn to predict its comings and goings, this is less true of those with anxiety disorders.

Anxiety manifests itself in countless ways. And the degree to which anxiety may disturb your daily functioning also varies widely. When anxiety causes a disruption in social and work activities, prevents you from carrying on daily tasks, or is simply always present, it may warrant treatment.

Some of the prominent forms of anxiety include:

- *Post-traumatic stress disorder*—Anxiety that disrupts behavior following a trauma.
- *Obsessive-compulsive disorder*—Persistent unwanted thoughts that produce anxiety, or actions that one feels driven to perform to alleviate this stress, but that may seem unusual, irrelevant, or silly
- *Phobias*—Recurrent fears of objects and activities that seldom, in themselves, are dangerous
- *Panic disorder*—Sudden and overwhelming fears of dying
- *Generalized anxiety*—Pervasive anxiety about almost anything that is new or different

The treatment of each of these problems is a bit different depending on what symptoms and impairments are present. A central theme to the effective treatment of all anxiety disorders or problems is exposure. This means you are re-exposed, on a regular basis, to the thing or things that produce anxiety, either directly or through directed imagery and imagination. Beyond this simple overriding characteristic in treatment, we are able only to describe the most typical aspects of established treatments for some of the most frequent anxiety-based conditions.

Post-Traumatic Stress Disorder

There are several specific variations of post-traumatic stress (PTSD) conditions whose nuances are largely irrelevant to our discussion here. The cardinal feature of all these conditions, however, is that they have occurred following an unusual, traumatic event. That event may be in the distant or recent past, but the symptoms include:

- Some combinations of flashback memories of the trauma
- Feelings of unreality (derealization) or of being outside your body, watching yourself engage in activities from a distance (depersonalization)
- Intrusive and spontaneous memories of the trauma
- Sleep disturbances, nightmares, or night terrors as well as anxiety attacks
- Withdrawal from friends or family, overreactions to any situation or event reminiscent of the traumatic event, and hypervigilance (increased sensitivity to environmental changes)

Such symptoms are a natural reaction to trauma and usually pass within weeks or a few months. Sometimes (approximately 30 percent of the time, partially depending on the severity of the trauma) they do not dissipate. These symptoms become established and resistant to change, and are often accompanied by depression.

You should remember, however, that these symptoms can occur for reasons other than exposure to trauma. In some people, they simply are the natural reaction to change. However, many clinicians believe that the presence of these symptoms invariably indicates that you have had a traumatic experience and may attempt to recover repressed memories of child abuse and the like. This conclusion has evoked considerable debate in scientific and practice circles about the advisability and need for treatment to seek a memory of a specific traumatic event when such symptoms occur. We hope that we have convinced you that inferring a specific cause from a general set of symptoms is a particularly dangerous and misleading practice. You should proceed very cautiously whenever a therapist suggests that you have repressed a trauma that needs to be uncovered for treatment to be successful.

The most frequently experienced and debilitating traumas are war experiences, auto accidents, rape, and childhood (sexual, emotional, or physical) abuse. The more chronic (long-standing) the anxiety symptoms, the more difficult the treatment. Traumatic response to war experiences is often especially difficult to treat since it is difficult to expose one to events, even in imagination, that are sufficiently similar to the original events to evoke a reenactment of the traumatic response.

Among those who develop a complex of PTSD symptoms, within a two-year period, only a minority (about 30 percent) have clinically significant symptoms. Some estimates of children who have been sexually assaulted indicate that from 70 to 80 percent are indistinguishable from their nonvictimized peers within a two- to three-year period. That doesn't lessen the seriousness and immorality of the acts nor are we shrugging off the horror to the children. We only wish to point out that children can overcome their symptoms and in most cases heal. Among those traumatized as adults, the percentage is a bit smaller, but still more than 50 percent of these individuals can overcome their symptoms without specific treatment within a relatively short time following the trauma.

As a rule of thumb, however, if symptoms dissipate they do so quite quickly and, if they do not, they become entrenched and require treatment. Within the first few months after trauma, treatment can speed amelioration, even among those whose symptoms would eventually dissipate on their own. If the debilitating and disruptive symptoms of anxiety remain beyond six or eight weeks, you should seriously consider entering treatment.

Treatments of PTSD and related trauma-induced conditions have advanced a great deal over the past several years. This is one of the great success stories in the mental health field.

BIOLOGICAL APPROACH

Biological treatments are based on the assumption that direct alteration of the subjective experience of anxiety will ameliorate overt symptoms of anxiety (e.g., sleep disturbance, flashbacks, intrusive thoughts, and so on). Clinicians believe that by lessening the symptoms, there will be an accompanying reduction of environmental cues evoking these fears. This removes the need for re-exposure to the events that originally evoked the anxiety. This assumption is partially correct.

The introduction of high potency anti-anxiety drugs has helped reduce the extent of symptoms such as sleep disturbances, flashbacks, intrusive thoughts, and derealization. Depersonalization is especially helped, at least in the short run, by these medications. However, medications do not seem to eliminate the need for re-exposure. Psychotherapy accomplishes both the task of reducing symptoms and altering the powers of environmental cues to evoke panic. The long-term resolution of entrenched PTSD symptoms and most other anxiety disorders is best achieved with re-exposure through psychotherapy. A combination of interventions from cognitive and behavioral models of intervention provides both symptomatic change and the clearest and probably most effective means of reducing the effect of anxiety cues in the environment.

COGNITIVE APPROACH

Aside from the general principle of exposing the patient to the original trauma and reactivating the emotions that were present at that time, there is another principle that guides effective treatment for traumatic reactions: Learning effective coping strategies. This reduces both symptoms and environmental cues. In Cognitive Therapy, the patient is taught skills for coping with reduced and disrupted sleep, intrusive thoughts, flashbacks, intense fear, and evoking events.

The principle of re-exposure means reliving and reactivating the level of arousal associated with the traumatic experience within a safe and predictable environment. To do this, the therapist may ask you to recall and describe the trauma in vivid detail, perhaps assisted by the introduction of visual imagery techniques and relaxation training by the therapist. With sufficient repetition, the level of anxiety associated with the recall of trauma dissipates, and with repetition and time it is quite likely to shrink enough that even those with very serious PTSD symptoms can live a relatively normal life.

The cognitive or skill training component of effective treatment follows guidelines similar to those suggested in the treatment of depression using cognitive-based interventions. This approach focuses on the symptom system in order to correct dysfunctional information processing. In applying these procedures, the therapist will help you identify the thoughts that precede or exacerbate anxiety. These thoughts relate both to a fear of the intrusive memory of the trauma, exaggerated fears of these circumstances recurring, and the terror of death and injury. Behind these fears, there may also be more general belief systems that are conducive to perpetuating the trauma. If you lived in an unstable or dysfunctional family, for example, you may have come to expect that every change is dangerous and this may magnify your reactions to crises.

Therapy for PTSD symptoms usually includes instruction and homework from the therapist that helps you to identify inaccuracies in your perceptions or beliefs, and to replace them with more accurate thoughts, and practice implementing these new thinking strategies. Those with PTSD frequently become particularly sensitive to their physical well-being (stomach pains, aches and pains, shortness of breath, dizziness) and prematurely anticipate that disastrous physical problems are besetting them. They tend to overinterpret and assume the worst.

You can expect that both the cognitive and behavioral therapist will be quite active, offer some guidance in how to manage stress reactions, help evaluate and problem solve, and will not spend a great deal of time trying to reevaluate your childhood. These therapists will ask you about your memories of the trauma. But if you do not recall them—common with sudden trauma such as automobile accidents—they will have you focus on the interpretations and expectations that you currently give these events when the symptoms become apparent. They will not seek to induce or recover memories if those memories are not already there.

Several other approaches, including the use of hypnosis, biofeedback, and acupuncture are common methods of helping you relax, but none has garnered sufficient evidence to permit any conclusion about their effectiveness.

Ordinarily, treatment will exert positive effects for about half of those who seek help within a period of three months, for over 80 percent of those who seek help within a period of twelve months. Treatment could continue for several years for the small percentage of people who have persistent problems beyond this point.

Both the extent and severity of PTSD can be complicated if there is a history of problems in interpersonal relationships, recurrent difficulties adjusting to changes in life, and previous episodes of depression or other types of anxiety. All these factors may lengthen the expected treatment.

OTHER APPROACHES

Conceivably, the type of exposure and reactivation of emotional arousal that is helpful in treating anxiety could occur in models of therapy that derive from the humanistic-experiential and psychodynamic models of behavior. Unfortunately, most therapists who use psychodynamic and experiential-humanistic approaches of behavior to develop their treatments rely on three cardinal and insupportable assumptions:

1. Everyone who has experienced certain types of trauma (especially sexual trauma in childhood) will have subsequent problems that require treatment.
2. The occurrence of past but specific traumas, particularly early sexual ones, can be identified even among those who have no recollection of them, by the presence of certain identifiable and distinguishing symptom complexes.
3. Long forgotten or recent traumas must be brought back to the patient through procedures designed to capture and restore these memories so they can be resolved.

These assumptions are, at best, insupportable from a scientific basis; at worst, they are patently false.

As we've noted, most people who experience trauma are extremely resilient. The symptoms following one trauma may be quite similar to those following another. Similar symptoms can occur without any specific trauma happening. There is no scientific evidence that recovering lost memories is either possible or necessary to help people cope with symptoms of PTSD.

Although it usually is helpful for patients to re-experience remembered traumas and bring their distress into focus, no specific evidence exists that where memories are inexact or lacking that they must be restored to induce maximal benefit. Indeed, there is evidence that doing so sometimes creates false memories—beliefs that certain events occurred when they did not—or produces more distress than it resolves.

Obsessive-Compulsive Disorder

Obsessions are mental images, impulses, or ideas experienced as intrusive, unwanted, and out of your control. Like the overt, evoking events of PTSD, the presence of internal events induces anxiety, distress, and other symptoms. Obsessions differ from simple worry by both their intrusiveness and our inability to control them through distraction or other means. They also differ from hallucinations in that you know they are self-created thoughts instead of externally generated ones. Knowing that obsessive thoughts come from inside you guarantees that they are disturbing.

A compulsion is a repetitive thought or behavior that is used to remove or relieve the anxiety arising from obsessive thoughts. Compulsions are performed to prevent some feared consequence. This thought or behavior feels out of your control and you engage in it routinely, even though it may appear foolish—even to you.

Often these anxiety-relieving thoughts and behaviors are unusual or inconsequential in their own right (checking or counting things) because they have no direct or logical connection to the unwanted, anxiety-producing thoughts or impulses. At other times, the anxiety-relieving acts or thoughts become problematic because of their excessive nature, or because it comes to feel necessary to engage in them, regardless of the appropriateness of the circumstances or their unusualness (praying, persistent hand washing, list-making, and so on). When such mental or behavioral acts are applied in a ritualistic, rigid fashion, and you come to think they are required for your safety, no matter how illogical, we call them "compulsions."

One of our patients, a former medical student, developed obsessive concerns with dirt and disease following exposure to dead bodies in an anatomy laboratory class. Her preoccupation prevented her from continuing school, and she soon found herself unable to walk on the floor without clean socks, unable to do laundry, and unable to wash dishes. Soon, she found that washing her hands or bathing relieved her anxiety. She came to feel obliged to bathe several times a day and to wash her hands fifteen or twenty times. Her hands became raw and infected because of the harsh soap, only motivating her to bathe more often. While she recognized that she was in no actual or unusual danger of contamination, she was not able to control these behaviors.

There are very effective treatments for obsessive and compulsive behaviors and thoughts. Empirically, the best-established and effective treatments derive from behavioral-cognitive models. Two central principles guide these treatments: response prevention and exposure.

The first, response prevention, is effective for treating compulsive behaviors. As a patient, you will be asked to delay engaging in a compulsive behavior or thought while you practice methods of control, relaxation, and redirection suggested by your therapist. As time progresses and your control increases, the length of this delay will increase, and you should finally be able to stop the compulsive behavior altogether. Delay and prevention of anxiety-reducing compulsions force both you and your body (from which you experience many anxiety-related symptoms) to learn other means of controlling anxiety.

Many people become fearful of going "crazy," losing control of impulses, or of dying if they do not engage in the anxiety-reducing compulsive behavior. Cognitive interventions, similar in nature to those discussed earlier for both depression and PTSD, can challenge these fears. Exposure to feared events and thoughts, through response delay and prevention, forces you to confront these fears and learn that they are not realistic.

It is imperative in all anxiety-related conditions that you learn both to have greater tolerance for the experience of anxiety and that *anxiety naturally goes away if you leave it alone.*

That may be the most important information a patient with anxiety disorder can learn. The usual, self-initiated efforts to avoid situations or otherwise engage in behavior designed to get rid of anxiety are unneeded and actually increase it: Simple tolerance and acceptance of anxiety allow it to dissipate. Anxiety always disappears once it is faced and tolerated; it becomes worse if you try to run from it.

Your therapist may ask you to see if you can make the anxiety happen by having certain thoughts or engaging in certain acts. Learning to relax while simultaneously experiencing this self-induced anxiety is often very helpful to those who fear choking or having a heart attack. Exercises in controlled breathing are helpful.

One of the authors once had a patient plagued by an obsessive impulse to stab his wife. He subsequently engaged in a process of compulsively avoiding knives or any place where they might be found—the kitchen, the dining room, the garage, certain bedroom drawers. His treatment involved identifying places and times in which these thoughts were most frequent, finding a "worry place" in those locations where he could sit and force himself to think the unwanted thoughts without engaging in compulsive avoidance. When the anxiety dissipated, he learned to relax himself and go about his regular activities.

The paradoxical instructions—to intentionally think about and bring to mind the thing that otherwise seemed to intrude unbidden upon his consciousness—demonstrated that doing so increased his ability to control the course of these thoughts. By bringing on the anxiety rather than by avoiding it with compulsive behaviors, this man established successful control of his obsessive thoughts and they finally disappeared.

Treatment of obsessions and compulsions will follow the general pattern seen with PTSD. About half of those who have these conditions can be treated effectively within about a six-month period, with another 30 percent responding within a year. Most contemporary treatments are structured to take place within ten to twenty-five sessions. If the program is well structured and if the patient does not have complicating conditions, this is enough time to satisfactorily address the needs of about 80 percent of those who enter such programs. Longer treatments of up to two years may be needed to alleviate the symptoms of those with more complex problems.

Procedures based on psychodynamic, interpersonal-systems, and humanistic-experiential models of behavior, including efforts to facilitate insight, discussions of early experience, uncovering inner conflicts, and disclosing interpersonal conflicts have not been found to be particularly effective for treating obsessive-compulsive patterns.

Phobias

Phobias are the third group of anxiety disturbances we discuss. Phobias are persistent fears, usually of specific objects, events, or circumstances. They range from fears of small animals, to fears of flying or being away from home, to fears of social contact. They also range in severity, with agoraphobia (fear of open spaces or of being away from home) being particularly disabling. People with social phobias fear being embarrassed or seek to avoid the negative appraisal of others. Other phobias are directed toward such activities as driving, flying, or public speaking.

In anticipation of encountering the feared event, object, or circumstance, the person with a phobia experiences a considerable amount of anxiety and frequently goes to unusual lengths to avoid the situation. If forced to confront the feared thing, the person becomes acutely anxious, and may even experience heart palpitations, sweating, dizziness, hyperventilation, and fears of dying or going crazy. You understand that your level of fear is excessive for the situation, even irrational, but that doesn't help.

The more specific the object or situation that provokes the phobia, the simpler the treatment. When our fears and phobias become widely generalized to the ordinary things we encounter in life—for instance, as happens in agoraphobia—life activities become impaired and treatment is much more complex and lengthy.

The most effective treatment programs derive from behavioral-cognitive models. Like all anxiety-based conditions, the central ingredient of the treatment is exposure. You must be exposed, repeatedly, to what you fear, to learn that the consequences are not as disastrous as you expect. In severe agoraphobia, especially if it's associated with panic attacks, medication may be helpful, but medication has side effects and the problems frequently return when the medication ends. Most research concludes that these symptoms can be effectively treated (more than 80 percent of the time) without medication.

Treatment of phobias of all types focuses on learning to tolerate being in the presence of the feared situation or object. One method of doing this is through the process of systematic desensitization, a procedure that reduces anxiety and phobic states by counter-conditioning with the use of relaxation. You will be trained to systematically relax your body, first in a safe environment and later (increasingly) in the presence of what you fear. Relaxation counteracts the anxiety, serving as something of an antagonist—you can't be relaxed and anxious at the same time.

Graded anxiety-producing events or objects are presented through visual imagery and description. This happens while you are in a state of relaxation, and the procedure is repeated until the image or memory of those stimuli no longer produce a state of anxiety. In presenting the feared stimuli, the therapist will first help you develop a fear hierarchy—a list of things and activities you are afraid of, progressing from least to most fearful.

In the systematic desensitization, descriptions of these events will be offered to your imagination while you are in a stage of relaxation, continuing from the least anxiety-arousing image through each step in the hierarchy. When all these situations can be imagined without any reported anxiety, the therapist may then ask you to begin trying out the procedure in the real world, exposing yourself to situations indicated on each step of the hierarchy, again proceeding from the least to the most anxiety-arousing situation.

In social phobia and agoraphobia, it is especially important to actually go where you fear to tread—buildings, planes, crowds, open spaces, and so on—first with others and later alone. You learn first, however, to attend to bodily sensations that signal the presence of anxiety, use a controlled breathing and muscle-tensing and relaxing antidote for anxiety, and stay put when fear arises and wait for it to dissipate. You learn to take small steps—don't try the big tasks until you've mastered the little ones—and often to let the "fear wash over you."

Treatments for most phobias, including the most complex—agoraphobia, have been so successful that some studies report that the majority of people with these conditions can successfully treat themselves by following the instructions in self-help manuals. Most bookstores have them.

These books present the above steps in a structured way, offering suggestions and guidance in the use of repetition and exposure and the process of learning to tolerate and manage anxiety without withdrawing from it. In applying such procedures, you will need to carefully evaluate and assess your progress. This involves measuring, at regular intervals, how close you can get to a feared object (and stay for the assigned time), how strongly you experience anxiety, and how often you avoid doing things you like because of the phobia. These measures provide benchmarks by which you can assess and even chart progress over time. Charting your progress can be an important motivator.

With phobias, research is quite clear in revealing that treatments that do not provide exposure and direct practice are not as effective as the program described here. Treatments based on models that view symptoms as being reflective of inner conflicts (psychodynamic models), those based on humanistic-experiential models of behavior, and those based on biological views of problems may all provide support and reassurance, but they are not as effective as behaviorally based interventions. Interpersonal-systems models of treatment may be helpful to the degree that they encourage you to explore new ways of coping with fear in the context of a supportive group of other people.

Treatment for phobias can also be quite short. Whether applied yourself, using a structured self-help book, or with the aid of a knowledgeable therapist, simple phobias of objects or activities (excluding agoraphobia) usually require fewer than ten sessions. Agoraphobia, uncomplicated by long-standing interpersonal problems or prior depression, usually requires from ten to twenty sessions, and even complex agoraphobia needs less than six months in most cases. This assumes, of course, that you have the motivation to do the difficult task of exposing yourself to feared situations.

Follow-up booster sessions are often recommended to reduce the likelihood of relapse. These are often scheduled on a monthly basis for some time after the major symptoms are alleviated, and may then be tapered off over the period of six to twelve months.

Panic Attacks

Panic attacks often occur simultaneously with phobias. Panic attacks are usually spontaneous, seem to be unprovoked, and are followed by persistent and intense worry in anticipation of having recurrent attacks.

In other words, you are terrified of being terrified.

With agoraphobia, you are afraid of having a panic attack in an unfamiliar place. Panic attacks vary in frequency but are so worrisome that people often don't know when they are better. A seventy-year-old patient, for example, sought help from one of us for what she called "panic attacks," though she had not had one in more than twenty years. She was certain she would have one if she didn't continue to organize her life to avoid it.

Panic attacks include strong physical distress, dizziness, shortness of breath, and heart palpitations. You become afraid that you cannot breathe, that you will die, or that some nameless doom is nigh. In fact, you can induce many of the symptoms of panic by hyperventilation. When you become afraid, or even anticipate having an attack, you may spontaneously begin to hyperventilate, thus bringing on a full-blown panic attack. People can often be cured by learning to control hyperventilation.

Panic attacks can also be successfully treated with some principles borrowed from behavioral models. Like the successful treatment of any anxiety, you have to learn to face and tolerate your fears. You have to let yourself be exposed to what you fear—in this case, the symptoms of panic itself. Self-induced panic brought on by hyperventilation can be used to help you establish a sense of control over the panic. This is not a self-directed treatment, however. It is necessary to do this under the guidance and assurance of a trained psychotherapist who can be available to aid you in the progressive nature of your efforts to control panic.

A particularly important aspect of treatment is the use of behavioral control procedures to transfer the control you develop to other situations in your daily life. Patients learn to control breathing, to relax, first in the therapist's office, and then to do those things in a variety of situations, including those that previously brought on the panic. Your therapist will help you learn to do "mini-relaxation" sessions, in which you tighten tense muscles and then relax them while exhaling evenly. People can usually learn to establish control over panic in this way in relatively few sessions (between five and fifteen) and can then learn to generalize and transfer this control to many other situations through continued practice.

Again, gaining insight into the nature of your early life or the symbolic or interpersonal value of your problems doesn't add to the effectiveness of these more direct treatment strategies. However, in early studies on treatments for panic and agoraphobia, psychodynamic treatments did as well as behavior-based ones for individuals who were very introspective, self-critical, socially fearful, and inhibited in emotional expression.

Generalized Anxiety

Generalized anxiety (GAD) is a collection of feelings, including excessive worry and distress that is experienced in a variety of situations. It is particularly provoked by the anticipation of social activities.

Fatigue, worry, difficulty concentrating, problems making decisions, muscle aches and pains, sleep disturbance—all may be experienced in GAD. And GAD may be felt in different situations, events, and circumstances—not just social activities like public speaking. GAD is not a phobia of some situation or activity, or the expectation of having a panic attack. It is, as the term implies, generalized to many situations and events.

Along with agoraphobia, generalized anxiety is arguably the most difficult of the anxiety disorders to treat. Treatment programs based on behavior-cognitive models seem effective with many people with this condition, but others respond to treatments derived from an experiential or psychodynamic model of behavior. To date, we do not know what makes these differences. The strongest research support is for a variety of cognitive treatments that help you identify your expectations and illogical fears that may be associated with various situations and develop ways of assessing more realistic and likely consequences. Making these explorations in the presence of a kind, supportive therapist who is able to listen and assist you in your explorations is also helpful.

You can expect that the therapist using behavioral methods will give you homework assignments and explore with you the nature of your thoughts before and after you experience anxiety. Keeping records of the situations and the intensity of your anxiety during the week will be important, as will a critical analysis of the nature of your thought patterns. Anxious individuals tend to have thought patterns that emphasize, unrealistically, the level of their responsibility for others' happiness, their achievement, and the quality of their performance. Often they become immobilized by these expectations and very self-critical if they fail to meet these excessive standards.

Some behavioral and cognitive procedures provide "stress-inoculation" for people who are prone to experience generalized anxiety. This procedure involves learning to recognize early physical and cognitive signals of stress and using coping strategies before the stress becomes too intense to manage well. Paying attention to the physical cues of anxiety as well as to the onset of unrealistic expectations helps you implement coping before the point when fear and anxiety are debilitating. With early prevention efforts, these procedures protect you from being overcome with anxiety.

Since generalized anxiety is so complex, the length of treatment is somewhat less certain than with such conditions as PTSD, phobia, or obsessive-compulsive anxiety. The nature of treatments is more diverse, and the role of early learning and experience more often become an important area of exploration. Exposure to the feared situation continues to be a common feature of treatment. But this often can be accomplished with psychodynamic or humanistic-experiential as well as by behavioral methods.

Health and Physical Reactions to Stress

At times, intense emotional distress or conflict can produce physical conditions or symptoms. Such problems have recently been the subject of considerable research. For some of these conditions—chronic pain, eating disorders, and sleep disorders—we have empirically established guidelines. Our discussion of treatment for them is somewhat less extensive, since the interventions used for treating these physical symptoms are similar to those used for treating depression and anxiety. Indeed, depression and anxiety are usually a part of the problem.

Chronic Pain

Pain is not a direct indication of a medical problem. It is the body's way of signaling the presence of physical danger. Even when the pain is associated with physical injury, your susceptibility to pain depends on how depressed you are, the suddenness of the injury, how tense you feel, and the response of others in your environment, along with the severity of any actual bodily injury.

You've read about football players who keep playing after breaking a leg or a nose, impervious to the pain until the game is over. Similarly, there are many instances of individuals, seriously injured in battle or in accidents, who save others, walk miles to find help, or carry on needed tasks without pain until the crisis is past. Then they collapse in agony.

The same individuals may howl if they got a splinter in their finger. The amount of experienced pain is as much a function of your expectations and circumstances as it is of the amount of actual tissue damage. We experience pain when a situation activates memories of prior painful experiences coupled with some kind of damage to the body, exciting an expectation that one is in danger of physical harm.

There are three well-established treatments for various types of chronic pain, representing treatments that derive from basic but different models of behavior.

Behavioral and cognitive models have been very effective in treating one form of chronic pain—headaches. Cognitive models have been useful in treating irritable bowel syndrome. Both cognitive and interpersonal-systems models are helpful in treating generalized and pervasive, chronic pain.

In the treatment of *headaches*, the first step is to understand patterns—when the headache begins and its accompanying symptoms. This is usually done by keeping a diary and making frequent ratings of both stress and headache pain. Tension headaches and tension-induced migraine headaches are responsive to relaxation training, similar to that produced in systematic desensitization. Cluster migraines and non-tension–induced migraines are also responsive to relaxation, but somewhat less so. The treatment most frequently prescribed for headache—drugs—as well as for other chronic and recurrent pain, derives from biological models of the problem, but their effects are uneven and often unpredictable. Moreover, there is a danger of becoming addicted to many of the common pain-relieving medications, so psychological interventions are often used both to relieve pain and to reduce drug dependence. Even if you do not become physically addicted to a pain medication, psychological dependence often occurs. You become convinced that you cannot manage pain without drugs and are loathe to give them up. Drug dependence and withdrawal effects unnecessarily complicate and lengthen treatment.

After tracking and observing patterns, the patient who applies behavioral and cognitive treatments for headaches learns to relax and visualize pleasant places and events to take his or her mind off the pain. Sometimes these relaxation procedures are supplemented by biofeedback, a method of increasing the relaxation of specific muscles by giving you direct auditory or visual feedback of how relaxed the targeted muscle is.

Hypnosis and self-hypnosis training can numb the sensation of pain and allow the therapist to make suggestions that deepen your ability to focus and relax. While we have criticized the use of hypnosis for recovering lost memories, here is an instance in which hypnosis is helpful. Several well-reasoned reviews of research indicate that hypnosis is very promising and often quite effective as a substitute for pain-killing drugs.

A third step in the treatment of chronic pain is the use of self-management and self-regulated relaxation. A skilled therapist can help you learn to use relaxation procedures at the first sign of headache in the hope of warding it off. If this is unsuccessful, the relaxation training can help you cope and manage the pain until it subsides. Muscle relaxation and sometimes hypnotic suggestions and meditation strategies to increase or decrease the circulation in the hands are used in migraine headaches to promote vasoconstriction, counteracting the vasodilation that causes headache pain. Vasoconstriction reduces migraine pain and interrupts the migraine headache cycle.

If you have *chronic and recurrent pain* in other parts of your body, such as back or stomach pain, the same general procedures work. However, the causes and treatments of these less-focused pains are often more complex than that of headaches. For example, it is not unusual for injured individuals to experience pain well after their bodies have healed. Their doctor may find no medical reason for the pain. By treating symptoms, your problem is compounded by the addition of drugs, which may leave you with intolerable cravings and cause you to become addicted. The pain may actually increase as your body learns to seek pain-killing drugs by developing more pain—a conditioned response—and the extent of debilitation can be quite extensive.

Treatment of these generalized pain reactions may begin in a hospital or partial hospital environment, especially if you are addicted or habituated to pain medications. Once there, the treatment starts with careful record keeping. You need to be weaned off pain-killing drugs, usually by getting a regularly scheduled "cocktail" in which the amount of medication is gradually reduced. The dissociation between the cocktail and the drugs fools your body into giving up its dependence. It extinguishes learned or conditioned pain by withdrawing the reinforcement—the pain killer.

While you are in the hospital, a final aspect of treatment will focus on your family. You will learn that well-meaning reactions by family members to your pain may actually increase or reward "pain behaviors." Family members will learn to let you do more things on your own and reward you for progress rather than for pain.

These are often difficult programs for patients because they mean withdrawing care, comfort, and addictive pain-killing medications at a time when they feel unable to take care of themselves and are susceptible to depression at the loss of their physical health. With the total family and health care system working together to provide a supportive and functional environment, however, you often can make substantial gains in the quality of living.

The characteristic symptoms of *irritable bowel syndrome* includes recurrent stomach aches and diarrhea that is recurrent and usually induced by stressful situations. The most helpful treatments are derived from behavioral models and often use cognitive skills training. By focusing on identifying unrealistic anticipatory fears, this method has been quite successful. Because depression is frequently present with these symptoms and because these anticipatory thoughts are similar to those found in depression, the treatment is very similar to that used in the cognitive treatment of depression. It is time limited, directed by the therapist, and seeks to address symptoms directly.

Cognitive therapy first works to identify automatic thoughts that occur with or in anticipation of the pain, and then helps you assess the unrealistic elements of these thoughts, replacing them with more realistic and less depressive thoughts. Its focus is on identifying thought patterns, usually ones that exaggerate the likelihood of bad consequences that induce anxiety, and then implementing procedures that correct erroneous thoughts. Part of the therapy includes practice of more realistic and less distressing thoughts. You learn to identify the triggers of physical symptoms, both in the environment and in your thoughts, and to employ both relaxation and self-talk to provide reassurance and correction.

Psychodynamic and experiential-humanistic treatments have also been reported to be effective with such problems, but research has not yet supported this claim.

Eating Disorders

Eating disorders include obesity (excessive weight gain), anorexia (excessive dieting and weight loss), and bulimia (binge eating and vomiting to control weight). To date, we have been quite unsuccessful in developing a lasting treatment for obesity or anorexia, but have achieved success in treating bulimia.

While many helpful programs are available for people who have either anorexia or obesity, relying usually on behavioral-cognitive and interpersonal models of behavior, *none has consistently produced reliable, lasting effects.* Diet, for example, is the most frequently used treatment for both conditions. However, lost or gained weight reverts to previous levels in a relatively short time. In fact, contemporary research has now demonstrated that dieting for either losing or gaining weight actually increases problems of weight maintenance rather than helping it by conditioning the body to tolerate wide variations of weight. In the case of obesity, for example, this means that the body learns to store increasing levels of fat for times of deprivation.

Both anorexia and bulimia are predominant among young, mid-dle-class women, especially in Western cultures. Bulimia is the most dominant of these conditions, but sometimes a person suffers both from anorexia and constricted food intake as well as bouts of binge-ing (overeating) and purging (vomiting)—bulimia.

Both conditions threaten your health, but anorexia can be espe-cially life threatening. The often severe loss of weight and compul-sive exercise that accompany this condition can deplete the body of resources needed to ward off disease, or shut down normal and need-ed body functions directly. People die from anorexia, as witnessed by the loss in recent years of several famous women gymnasts and the singer Karen Carpenter.

Both disorders have been treated with systemic behavioral and cognitive methods, including the reinforcement of appropriate eat-ing habits and weight management as well as the identification of illogical or irrational thought patterns. Family members have been included in the treatment in an effort to change the role of food in the expression of family emotions and in offering rewards for appro-priate food ingestion. These treatments have demonstrated some short-term benefits, but few lasting gains.

Although they are not impressive concerning anorexia and obesi-ty, treatments based on cognitive and interpersonal models of expe-rience are effective in treating those with bulimia, and interventions based on behavioral models have shown some promise, though any conclusions are still tentative. Other treatments are marginally suc-cessful or produce such widely inconsistent results that they have failed the test of replication—an important test of treatment success. Both cognitive therapy and interpersonal therapy for bulimia close-ly follow the procedures that have been effective in the treatment of depression. In fact, IPT, in particular, is virtually unchanged when used to treat bulimia. IPT deals with central conflicts, including the problems of grief, skill deficits, interpersonal disputes, and role tran-sitions.

In applying cognitive therapy, the procedures are similar to those used for treating depression, but homework assignments frequently focus directly on eating rituals. A component of treatment usually involves communication training with significant others in the patient's life.

Interventions based on behavioral and cognitive-behavioral models of problems take one of three tactics:

1. To address eating binges and purges as habits that are maintained by a system of rewards, by removing or changing the rewards.
2. To attempt to reduce levels of interpersonal discord assumed to serve as conditioned cues that stimulate bulimic symptoms.
3. To reduce levels of anxiety that are also assumed to provoke bulimia.

Treatments based on the first two tactics both identify binge eating as the primary focus of treatment. The third tactic identifies the experience of anxiety as the target, viewing it as a mediator of the problem.

In the first, binge eating serves as an index of a lack of knowledge and skill that prevents patients from maintaining normal weight and adhering to a normal diet. Binge eating could be the patient's response to failing to control weight successfully with her usually poorly planned diets. In this treatment, individuals receive information about dietary management and practice in applying it to any weight problems. You are given material to read, along with weight and nutrition charts, and are monitored as you practice developing and maintaining a diet. These procedures are also common in treating anorexia, but with somewhat less success.

Therapists also believe that the patient regulates her emotions and manages her relationships with others by binge eating. The treatment teaches her more adaptive ways of relating to and coping with others. She learns the skills of listening and communicating, and is instructed in how to relieve interpersonal stress in ways that do not include food. Again, the patient in these treatments will record behaviors, eating and purging activities, and interpersonal interactions. She will receive instruction and practice, through role playing, in how to interact with others.

The remaining tactic used by behavioral-based interventions is to target anxiety as the condition to be changed, rather than directly focusing on bulimia itself. In this approach, vomiting is seen as a compulsive behavior that serves the same reinforcing function as hand washing or counting in obsessive-compulsive conditions—it reduces anxiety. You are asked to delay vomiting and tolerate the anxiety while anxiety situations are presented, first through imagining them and then in actual situations. Delay of symptoms increases as tolerance is extended, until bulimia stops altogether.

In each of these interventions, a patient being treated for bulimia can expect the therapist to be very active, to educate as well as to understand, and to provide homework assignments that facilitate the process of self-inspection.

The course of treatments for bulimia and anorexia are usually substantially longer than that for depression (frequently lasting a year or more), but the similarity of treatment models, applications, and even goals provides a testament to depression as a common denominator in eating disorders.

Sleep Disorders

Sleep disturbances are present when you either have too much or too little sleep, or when you are awake when you want to be asleep or asleep when you want to be awake.

Most people are familiar with insomnia, a condition defined as the inability to fall sleep or stay asleep when it is appropriate, but they don't usually think of excessive sleepiness or sleepiness and wakefulness at the wrong times as a problem. Most of us have feelings of sleepiness several times each day. We also occasionally have trouble falling asleep. But for either excessive sleepiness or insomnia to be problems in need of treatment, they must interfere with our ability to perform daily activities requiring concentration and organized thought.

That usually means that the insomnia leaves us sleepy and unable to focus during the day. Despite how well one may sleep at night, some persons with a problem of excessive sleepiness periodically will have "attacks" of sleep—unpreventable periods of nodding off, even in the middle of conversations, while conducting business, or being otherwise engaged. One condition of excessive sleepiness is called narcolepsy.

Both conditions—insomnia and narcolepsy—can be the result of medical problems, medications, or emotional stress and depression.

They also can be "primary" disturbances—they can exist all on their own, independent of any known medical or psychological condition.

With narcolepsy, for example, a person suddenly feels compelled to sleep even though they didn't feel sleepy a moment ago and may have been active. Narcolepsy is a neurological, not a psychological condition, however, and it responds well to medication. There is no well-established psychological treatment that corrects this condition, although many doctors, when confused about the condition, may label people who have it as being "depressed" and refer them for psychological treatments. Appropriate psychological management provides education about the condition and help in learning to adjust daily activities to minimize the impact of the condition on work and interpersonal activities. The best advice for individuals suffering from narcolepsy is to see a physician.

Another disorder of excessive sleepiness, apnea, can be very frightening because sufferers stop breathing during a portion of each night's sleep. This, too, is a physical problem. Diagnosis of this condition, and its treatment, requires considerable medical expertise.

Insomnia, on the other hand, has more general causes than sleep apnea or narcolepsy. It appears as a part of many different conditions. Medical problems, life changes, prescription drugs (even sleeping pills), depression, anxiety, and almost any tension can induce insomnia. Unlike apnea or narcolepsy, however, insomnia is relatively easy to diagnose and, in most cases, is responsive to self-directed treatment even when it's part of other conditions.

While it is usually helpful to have a medical opinion, the treatment for most cases of insomnia is simple and you can do it yourself. It is based on a behavioral model and includes the following steps:

1. Get up at the same time each day, regardless of how badly you slept the night before.
2. Don't try to correct the problem by going to bed earlier. Go to bed at your regular time, but only if you're sleepy.
3. Control the room environment to maintain a cool temperature, a constant humidity, and a diminished, background sound. Static from a radio set between stations often provides this

"white noise" without disrupting sleep the way voices and music may.

4. Use your bed only for sleeping. Do your reading and TV watching in other parts of the house.
5. Never *try* to go to sleep. If you don't fall naturally to sleep within twenty minutes after either awakening during the night or when going to bed, get up and read, write, or relax in another part of the house until you are sleepy again.
6. Stop smoking and drinking. Alcohol, tobacco, coffee, soft drinks, and tea are all stimulators and reduce or fragment sleep.
7. Give yourself time. This routine may take up to two weeks before you are reset on a regular schedule. If after this time, the problem has not improved and you've followed these rules faithfully, check with your doctor for a referral to a sleep or mental health specialist.

If you are one of those people who do not respond to self-directed treatment, you can still expect that these guidelines will still be part of what a knowledgeable mental health professional will prescribe. Medications may also be used, but only for the short run. Sleeping pills are often addictive and usually reach a point (often within a month) when they interfere more with sleep than help it. There are few instances when one should come to rely on sleep medication beyond a few weeks.

One exception is when the sleep problem is part of depression or other serious psychological problems, and the medication is used to treat this serious condition. Antidepressants—drugs to reduce levels of depression—and medications that improve the ability to think logically may all improve sleep as a side effect of helping these other problems. Beyond the use of interventions designed to improve sleep, other behavioral, cognitive, or interpersonal interventions have been used in treating insomnia, but none has proved more effective than this self-directed treatment.

Relationship and Sexual Problems

In a recent survey of psychotherapy's effects among a sample of *Consumer Reports* readers, marital and relationship therapists were judged to be the least effective and helpful. Empirical literature on these topics is somewhat more optimistic, but the reactions of those who have experienced these treatments emphasize some important points. When people are engaged together as a family or couple in explorations of themselves and their needs, they often change at different rates. Sometimes, perhaps more often than not, at least one of them becomes more distant and less dependent on the other. If your self-esteem is benefiting in some way from being depended on and "needed," discord will almost certainly arise. So, it's almost a given that a large number of the people treated for relationship problems will be unhappy with the results, no matter how good these results are for everyone else.

Research indicates that successful treatments are available for both marital discord and for correcting problems of sexual performance.

Marital Discord

If psychotherapy results in one person's feeling more self-confident and desirous of seeking her or his goals while the other remains dependent, one will be happy and one will not. For one, dissolution of the marriage may be a demonstration of the therapy working, but for the other, it will show how it failed.

Although there is some dispute about the level of support offered, we believe that three models of marital therapy have received adequate support from sound empirical research to conclude that they are probably effective for treating marital discord. A variant of one of these has also been successfully applied to the specific problems presented by sexual dysfunction.

Psychodynamic marital therapy assumes that the frustrated inner wishes of each partner are enacted within the relationship in a way that is similar to the earlier relationships that one had with parents. In the process of trying to rework old family conflicts through the relationship with our marital partners, we inadvertently cast them in the role of our parent. We then fight old battles and assume infantile roles in a vain hope that the resolution will be different in this version of the old and recurrent play.

Treatment derived from a psychodynamic approach seeks to identify the unspoken wishes and fears that are being expressed in these relationships and uncover their nucleus in early childhood relationships. Couples are encouraged to reflect, evaluate their family rules and hidden agendas, identify a pattern that pervades their interpersonal relationships, and recognize which of their childhood needs and fears they may have brought into the marriage. A major focus is on improving the nature and honesty of communication. The marriages and relationships of parents, grandparents, and even great-grandparents frequently are topics of discussion in an effort to find the family patterns of conflict to which the various marital partners are responding.

The patient in such treatment can expect the therapist to vary his or her response, sometimes being quite silent, at other times quite instructive and interpretive. The treatment may last a year or more, although short-term interventions with more limited goals sometimes work (fewer than forty sessions). Between sessions, patients are encouraged to reflect and talk with one another. Homework assignments are few.

Marital therapy derived from a behavioral approach is a short-term intervention that attempts to alter reinforcement patterns between marital partners. Therapists using this model are very active and try to develop communication skills and knowledge in their patients so they can gain rewards through their relationship with their spouse. The therapist is instructive. Homework assignments are introduced to encourage the couple to work together on joint projects, talking and listening during disagreements, and gathering information designed to enhance each person's knowledge of the other. You will be asked to monitor your feelings, learn to listen while inhibiting your impulse to respond, take alternative viewpoints, and negotiate behavioral contracts.

Contracting, or what behaviorists call "behavioral exchange," is an especially important part of this therapy. It is a system in which each partner must identify certain behaviors they want from their partner. These behaviors are exchanged as a form of bartering in a negotiated contract. The therapist mediates this process and couples keep records to prevent unfairness. For example, a male partner who wants more sex may negotiate and agree to give his wife more romantic time in exchange.

Sometimes, a variant of these contracts begins with learning to use a system of rewards that helps people identify when they are doing things that are irritating or rewarding to their partner. The use of plastic tokens to cue such behaviors sometimes takes pressure off the tendency to get into heated discussions. Contracts structure and define roles, develop expectations, and ensure that each partner takes personal responsibility for progress in treatment.

Psychodynamic and behavioral marital therapies have been systematically compared among maritally distressed couples. Interestingly, they were found to be effective and to yield equivalent effects on marital satisfaction after about twenty sessions. However, several years after therapy, substantial differences in divorce rates were noted. Those couples who underwent psychodynamic marital therapy were several times more likely to stay married than those who engaged in behavioral marital therapy.

Emotionally focused marital therapy is a third model of couples therapy and derives from an experiential-humanistic model of behavior. In this approach, marital relationships improve by effectively communicating feelings and increasing the intensity and awareness of the marital partner's feelings. It is assumed that feelings become blocked by fears of expression, many remaining from early parental experiences.

The therapist using this model encourages direct dialogue about expectations and fears, frequently inviting each partner to imagine that their parents are in the room and can express their satisfactions and fears about the patient or partner. Dialogues with imagined but important family members help patients recognize their wants and expectations and possibly learn the origin of these desires. Patients who felt a sense of closure regarding these past relationships seemed to benefit the most from this therapy. The intensity of marital conflict as well as personal unhappiness were both lessened.

Sexual Dysfunction

Behavioral sex therapy is a behavioral form of treatment specifically employed in treating both men and women who have had difficulty with sexual performance.

Orgasmic dysfunction in women, the inability of a woman to achieve orgasm during sexual intercourse, has been improved by a treatment that teaches the patient's partner to provide stimulation without demand or expectation of intercourse. Using a vibrator and manual stimulation, first controlled by the female patient and then with increasing control by the male partner, increases the likelihood of an orgasmic response as well as the rewarding power of intercourse.

Male erectile and ejaculatory dysfunction, an inability to achieve or maintain an erection or the inability to control ejaculation, is also responsive to behaviorally based treatments. These treatments focus on increasing the patient's arousal and control by fantasy, erotic reading and pictures, videos, and manual stimulation by a partner. Erections improve when the male partner is encouraged to relax and let go of his usual need to please his partner, allowing himself to be stimulated. The treatment program for erectile problems ordinarily takes approximately ten to thirteen weeks and consists of a series of progressively complex acts leading to intercourse. During the treatment, the male remains dependent on the female partner for providing the direction and stimulation.

Homework tasks proceed from an initial stage of nondemand sexual pleasuring to tasks that facilitate sexual arousal and ejaculation outside the vagina. The tasks include containing the penis within the vagina, moving within the vagina, and, finally, ejaculation within the vagina. Only then is the male partner encouraged to begin to take a more active role in initiating sexual responses. Reciprocally, the male is expected to also pleasure his partner in a nondemanding, non-intercourse method while treatment is continuing.

Male ejaculatory difficulties, the inability to ejaculate or failure to delay ejaculation, are also treated with a behavioral approach. The procedure is symptom focused and progressive.

For the male who ejaculates prematurely, the treatment emphasizes developing greater tolerance for stimulation by building toward an erection without intercourse, but then stopping the stimulation and allowing the erection to dissipate several times before permitting ejaculation. This process gradually increases the patient's tolerance for stimulation and the ability to maintain the erection over time. Only when he has demonstrated that he can achieve and then maintain the erection several times is ejaculation allowed. Once he achieves control without sexual intercourse, penetration is then initiated using the same progression of steps.

Males who cannot ejaculate are treated somewhat differently, with the major focus on increasing pleasure and arousal through imagery, nondemand pleasuring, and stimulating materials. The key, again, is the development of progressive homework tasks that relieve performance pressures and only gradually introduce actual intercourse.

While these sexual procedures are effective, most sexual problems reflect the co-occurrence of some type of relationship problem, a loss of sexual interest, or a partner who has different wants and expectations. Effective treatment for a couple with many different problems, therefore, may combine a behavioral treatment for sexual dysfunction, and either an interpersonal, psychodynamic, or behavioral-cognitive treatment for marital discord and communication. That means the success of treatments for sexual difficulties cannot be disentangled from the successful treatment of a disturbed relationship.

GUIDELINES TO KEEP IN MIND

As we have described the treatments for different kinds of problems, you may have noted that many effective treatments derive from a behavioral-cognitive or interpersonal-systems model of behavior.

Specific models, identified as cognitive therapy or interpersonal psychotherapy, have been widely applied and are frequently successful with a wide array of problems. Relatively few problems have been found to be responsive to treatments based solely on psychodynamic, experiential-humanistic, and biological approaches. In the case of psychodynamic therapies and biological ones, this is not because of a lack of research. We conclude from the research available that psychodynamic treatment is effective only for a relatively select set of problems. It is helpful in treating rather broadly based problems that are manifest as depression and marital discord. Psychodynamic treatment is not remarkably successful for focal symptoms and problems, such as those that are present in anxiety disorders, health-related disorders, and sexual dysfunction.

In contrast, biological treatments are quite effective with specific symptoms. They work well in alleviating the symptoms of depression, are more limited in addressing the symptoms of anxiety, and, in the short-term, work for sleep and health-related psychosocial problems.

The relatively limited variety of conditions and symptoms for which humanistic-experiential–based therapies have been found to be effective is somewhat different. The failure of treatments based on these models to appear in lists of demonstrably effective treatments for different problems probably reflects the absence of research. When researched, they have often been successful. Current research suggests that they are effective ways of treating depression, marital discord, and perhaps some kinds of medical-related problems.

One should note that some recent, innovative therapies used for anxiety and depression, such as Thought-Field Therapy and Eye Movement Desensitization, are not listed in our recommendations because research is lacking or unclear.

It is disconcerting that the treatments whose effects have been most clearly demonstrated are among the least used in clinical practice, while those with the fewest demonstrable effects are among the most frequently practiced. As a consumer, the wide disparity between what is effective and what is practiced means that it is very likely you will be subjected to a treatment that is less than demonstrably effective.

This is a serious matter, and talking it over with your therapist is not likely to help. Therapists tend to be very protective of their practices and are reluctant to develop new interventions simply to satisfy the desires of a particularly educated patient.

Our recommendations:

* If your problem is depression, generalized anxiety, or marital discord, a variety of effective treatments are available. If you like and feel

understood by your therapist, benefits are likely. If not, find such a therapist with whom you are compatible.

* If you have a specific and disruptive symptom, such as those related to most anxiety disorders, health-related symptoms, sleep problems, or sexual problems, then the specific nature of the treatment may be more important. In these instances, failure to improve may be either because an ineffective treatment is being used or the problem is different and more complex than you have thought.

* Start by discussing the issue with your therapist and see if you can identify whether the treatment being applied fits the general descriptions that we have provided here. If not, then an outside opinion may be helpful and a change of treatment or therapist necessary.

* If you are not enjoying the benefits of treatment, discuss this with your therapist and get a second opinion about whether treatment is proceeding as expected. This may help resolve your concerns about the progress of treatment.

Therapists who are most familiar with and prone to use scientifically supported treatments are often full-time faculty members at universities, within departments of psychology, education, or psychiatry. Call your local university and explore these avenues until you find someone you can talk with in a caring atmosphere and from whom you can obtain treatments that fit your problem and personality.

As you select a therapist or as you anticipate changing therapists, you should keep in mind other considerations:

* Conducting interviews and experiencing a few sessions of treatment should provide information that will allow you to compare your experience with the suggested guidelines described in this chapter.

* You should discuss your concerns first with your therapist and give his or her impressions and comments careful consideration. If you decide on a second opinion, it may be useful to seek someone other than another professional recommended by your therapist. Get a referral from your priest or rabbi or your family doctor. Let the new

Therapies for Various Problems

Disorders	What Works	Questionable
Major depression	Biological/Pharmaceutical Behavioral Cognitive Interpersonal Psychodynamic	
Post-traumatic stress syndrome	Biological Behavioral-Cognitive	Humanistic-Experiential Psychodynamic
Obsessive-compulsive	Behavioral-Cognitive Biological	
Phobias	Behavioral-Cognitive	
Panic attacks	Behavioral	Psychodynamic
Generalized anxiety	Behavioral-Cognitive Psychodynamic Humanistic-Experiential	
Chronic pain	Behavioral Interpersonal	Biological/Pharmaceutical
Irritable Bowel syndrome	Cognitive	
Obesity[a]	[c]	Behavioral-Cognitive
Anorexia[b]		Behavioral-Cognitive
Bulimia	Cognitive Interpersonal Behavioral Humanistic-Experiential	
Sleep disorder	Behavioral Biological/Pharmaceutical	
Sexual dysfunction	Behavioral-Cognitive Interpersonal	

[a] There is no proven therapy for obesity.
[b] There is no proven therapy for anorexia.
[c] Obesity, anorexia, and bulimia all have a component of depression that can specifically be treated. See treatments for depression.

178

clinician know that you want an opinion and are not, at this time, seeking to change therapists. Discuss your concerns frankly, but don't make a premature commitment to change therapists until you've had time to think it over carefully.

We've developed a chart for you that matches disorders with what science tells us works. Again, keep in mind that, for most problems, simply having someone sit and listen to you will work for most people most of the time. The chart is for those with either no access to such support or who are more seriously affected and need serious professional treatment. Besides listing what we know works, we have also occasionally pointed out things we don't believe work well.

If a therapy is not listed in the chart, it means there is no scientific basis for accepting that the treatment is effective. That is not the same as saying it doesn't work. It might work; there simply is no hard evidence. Also keep in mind that for many disorders, such as depression, combinations of therapies are sometimes more effective than single treatments.

1. The metaphors of mental illness and addiction most often used to identify and diagnose those with emotional distress and behavioral disorders do not consistently fit the nature of these disturbances.
2. By looking at theories that guide treatment as immutable truths instead of as working assumptions, the development of effective treatments is hampered.
3. Science and empirically derived knowledge afford protection to the therapist and to the patient from the biases that arise from unverified models of behavior.

The Notion of Illness and Diagnostic Labeling

We probably would not be writing this book had Freud not applied his metaphor of illness to the subjective, abstract, unobservable consequences of normal experience. (See Chapter 5.)

Western societies have demonstrated a gift for thinking about different behaviors as illnesses. There seems to be no end to the diagnostic labels we have been able to create and the treatments we propose to ameliorate them. The medicalization of behavior has been abetted, for better or for worse, by the incorporation of mental health care into the domain of health insurance and managed care systems.

There appears to be a universal tendency of human societies to take examples and metaphors that work reasonably well in one situation and apply them to everything with a hint of similarity. Perhaps this too is a disease—*metaphor expansionitis*. The expansion of the list of diseases has continued without regard for whether these new illnesses are simply extreme examples of normal behaviors, products of experience and choice, or reflect some actual change and malfunction of physical structure. Unfortunately, there was not then, nor is there now, a reliable method for determining what behaviors are volitional and arise from normal processes, and which are not and do not.

The case of addiction is a good example of *metaphor expansionitis*. There is no question that certain chemicals produce physical dependence and addiction. They change and damage physical structures. Addiction is marked by two major characteristics: (1) physical habituation in which bodily function requires increasing levels of the substance; and (2) physical changes associated with withdrawal.

This concept of addiction as a disease fits the cases of opiates, tobacco, caffeine, alcohol, and many other substances. By extending the concepts of habituation and withdrawal to the realm of subjective experience, however, the list of addictions has now far exceeded the bounds of logic and helpfulness. Any behavior or inner experience that feels out of one's personal control (habituation), and is followed by sadness and fear (withdrawal) when expected events cease, is now an addiction. Nothing need be introduced from outside; indeed, the addictive substance may exist within the person who has the disease. Sex addiction, gambling addiction, food addiction, and many others are examples in which the metaphor of illness does not fit well. There is no injected substance, no physical habituation, no chemical dependence.

That the body craves food or that individuals desire love and suffer certain emotional consequences when their wants are not realized is not grounds for calling something an addiction. It is a normal process of events in the face of frustrated expectancies. To call it a disease trivializes those things that represent true malfunctions of the body; it also distorts the meaning humans derive from love and other emotional responses.

Some dangers that arise from this tendency to externalize illnesses—to carve them out of uncomfortable feelings, unwanted behaviors, or unacceptable conduct that are even modest departures from normal experience—trapped George Franklin. Here, symptoms of his daughter's distress, without regard for whether they were normal responses to volitional events or involuntary ones, were viewed as symptoms of a disease. Once the metaphor of disease erupts, the search for a specific pathogen to account for its symptoms is both logical and justified. Any question of its value or validity becomes moot. A nonexistent disease of the mind caused by a nonoccurring pathogen of exposure to early sexual and physical abuse apparently was created in the mind of the therapist and her patient. A specific treatment is indicated and a professional is duty bound to treat the condition.

We see in this example how the indiscriminate use of labels that offer artificial explanations of behavior invokes the need for treatment and transfers the blame for the behavior to someone or something else. Blame is passed to the society, the family, the illness, one's experience, and sometimes even to the patient. In those cases in which there is not a true malfunction of a physical structure, transferring such blame and responsibility probably does little to correct the situation.

Expressing Myths in Mental Health Treatment

In the past 100 years, an explosion of knowledge and dramatic changes in society has occurred. The car and airplane have replaced the horse and buggy, electricity has replaced the candle, centralized air and heat have replaced the fireplace and fan, actual space travel has replaced Jules Verne and Flash Gordon, and mass manufacturing has replaced the family cottage industry.

And therapists have replaced priests and family sages.

As the assigned healers and priest-confessors for a host of created and real societal and personal ills, modern mental health practitioners have sought to develop interventions for alleviating these ills. These interventions are each based on a particular conception or model of how people function and change.

No single model of behavior is true or effective for treating all problems and individuals. Treatments from each model are effective for some problems and situations, and ineffective or less effective for others. This observation might logically be expected to result in different patients and problems being treated with different models of intervention. Astonishingly, this does not happen. Instead, mental health practitioners continue to adopt a single theoretical model and offer treatments based on it to all patients who are so fortunate or unfortunate as to walk through their doors.

Both Ms. Franklin and her therapist adhered to an explicit theory based on concepts of psychic conflict and the protective functions of forgetting (repression). The therapist was led by the theory that Ms. Franklin's positive feelings toward her father were irreconcilable with the assumed observation of the atrocious act of murder. The only avenue of protection from this conflict was repressing the unacceptable memory. All well and logical—and wrong. More important, the treatment to correct the nonexistent problem was also wrong and dangerous.

The typical methods used to deal with psychic conflict in psychodynamic approaches include dream interpretation and free association. The use of such reality-bending procedures as hypnosis is known to be unreliable for extracting factual events from memory. Under hypnosis, people tend to create stories and present them as facts in an apparent effort to please others. They frequently believe what they present. That's why hypnosis is banned from use as evidence in California courts.

The decision of Ms. Franklin's therapist to use such procedures for such a questionable purpose may have arisen from several sources. One may have been a too-firmly affixed commitment to a psychodynamic explanation of the anxiety and sleep disturbances that brought Ms. Franklin to treatment. Reliance on firmly believed theory, rather than on objective knowledge about causes and consequences, may have guided the therapist to use this tactic, testify on behalf of Ms. Franklin, and allow the patient to misrepresent the conditions under which the memories were recovered. We believe we see in these descriptions some of the indicators of boundary violation described in Chapter 4.

While behavioral difficulties are usually described through a medical or biological model of disease, treatments rely on many more diverse models. The mere disparity between the concepts and analogies we use to describe and diagnose problems, on one hand, and those we use to treat them, on the other, should alert us to how poorly the disease metaphor fits human conditions of suffering.

In the 1970s, it seemed logical and practical to extend health insurance coverage to the arena of emotional suffering. At that time, the human growth movement was at its peak, and all unhappiness was considered the product of inner dysfunction. You couldn't throw a beer can out of a dormitory window without hitting a psychology major, and there was an optimistic hope that psychological awareness would provide a correction to all social and personal ills. But this optimism was not justified, and the costs of treating an exploding list of diseases with an expanding array of health service providers became onerous.

The disparity of arguing for and against an illness model at the same time, may have been one of the major reasons why mental health coverage has come under such fire by third-party payers and politicians. In the 1970s, psychology made the mistake of arguing against the medical model, emphasizing that behavior was learned not diseased, and at the same time insisting that health insurance programs should cover these services. Surprisingly, legislation was passed despite this logical contradiction. In this process, psychological intervention became fixed on treating rather than preventing disease.

Contemporary research suggests that the greatest benefit of psychological knowledge to modern health care may not be in its use to treat the multitude of manufactured and real diseases, but in reducing the risk of future suffering and dysfunction following physical disease and personal loss. Psychological principles and science have much to offer our changing high-risk lifestyles, by decreasing dangerous behaviors and alleviating the suffering caused by a chaotic and stressful environment.

We have pointed out the abuses, misdirected uses, and misuses of mental health theories, not to disparage them or their value. We all operate according to theories, and they are important in our lives. It also is true that when applied to public needs, these theories must be explicit and formal. This formality facilitates their use and provides a degree of correction for logical errors through discourse and debate. But when the theories we use are factually incorrect, rather than simply logically incorrect, failure to change them could be disastrous.

Because they are outside the scope of most of our abilities to either prove or disprove them, it is not surprising that both the implicit and explicit theories of mental health practitioners have occasionally damaged people's lives. Indeed, it is surprising to us that psychology and psychiatry have done so much good and so little harm, given both the pervasiveness of our resistance to questioning our assumptions and the ambivalent attitude with which we have treated the question of efficacy.

The Protective Potential of Science

Scientific methods require that causal relationships be demonstrated independently of those with a vested interest in proving the presence of that relationship. Scientists use measures of symptoms and causes that do not depend on the theorist—and provide descriptions of methods that can be used by others to replicate their findings. Unless findings can be replicated on different patients, in different situations, by different clinicians, the evidence is suspect and considered tentative.

None of the different models of behavior has risen to the top as having a lock on the truth. Most of their assumptions cannot be adequately tested. When we apply scientific tests to their effects, as represented in treatment outcomes, the evidence indicates that all have won and must have prizes. Yet different approaches are effective with different populations of patients and for different types of problems.

A patient may be protected from ineffective, ignorant, malicious, and dangerous therapy practices by obtaining knowledge about the therapist and the scientific support that guides the treatment being used. A patient who is in possession of this knowledge will enjoy some protection from therapists who have kept their theories intact, despite evidence that may question them. So, how can you obtain this knowledge?

Often patients must make decisions about their care when they don't have adequate information. This is particularly critical at two points. The first is when you initially seek help. The second crucial point is when you attempt to evaluate whether the treatment you have received is working.

Seeking Help

As you come to identify a source of emotional or situational pain and conflict, you may have many fears and doubts about seeking treatment. When you consider the prospect of treatment, remember several points.

- Most people who enter mental health treatment benefit from it in a reasonable time. Some even get better just by making an appointment.

- Most of those who offer such treatment are responsible and ethical.
- Most of the positive effects of treatment derive both from your motivation and your willingness to consider and try new options in your life.
- The therapist's primary contribution is the invitation he or she provides for you to explore, consider, and try.

Once you get by the hurdle of deciding to get treatment, the next step is finding a therapist who can help you. In searching out such an individual, there are other factors to remember.

- Obtain a list of four or five names from your family physician and especially from acquaintances and friends who have had successful treatment experiences.
- Check the therapist's credentials by making a call both to their office and to the relevant board of licensing. Ask about licenses and inquire if the prospective therapist has ever been censured by the board.

Obtaining a list of names is important because each therapist is different. Someone who knows you, such as your doctor, or is similar to you, such as a close friend, may help narrow the field. Those who have had a successful treatment experience are a good reference point to help ensure that you too receive beneficial treatment.

A check on the therapist's credentials does little to tell you if the practitioner is competent, but it will help you avoid the fraudulent therapist or one who has been sanctioned for unprofessional conduct.

Once you have obtained a list, then it is time to interview prospective practitioners just as you would interview any prospective employee. You can do this by phone or in person, though it is likely that the practitioner may charge you for the time. As you initiate the interviews, particular information will be especially useful.

The most crucial consideration is finding someone you respect and like and who seems to listen and care about what happens to you.

It is important that you find a therapist whose theoretical views seem logical and reasonable to you. Avoid those whose views do not make sense and that seem strange and foreign.

Evaluating Your Progress

Compatibility does not necessarily mean similarity. In fact, research has demonstrated that differences in key beliefs between patients and therapists makes change more likely. Apparently, we don't just need to be assured that our viewpoints are right, but we benefit from some kind of confrontation with the probability that there are other ways to view the problem. Therefore, there may be occasions when you are best served by developing a new view of your behavior and your life. It may be useful to be challenged. For example, to overcome depression, you might benefit from coming to see that bad events are less permanent than you thought, infrequent, and caused by many things—not just your own behavior. It might be helpful, therefore, if your therapist presented and believed in this contrasting viewpoint. But the concepts used by the therapist must make sense to you and the way you think about the world.

Simplistically, psychotherapy is effective when the patient can be persuaded to change beliefs and viewpoints, alter behavior, or modify feelings. Change is a broad term; it can vary from learning to accept one's self or another person, to making a major change in life roles and activities.

In effecting these changes, psychotherapy shares procedures with other types of social persuasion and influence. Psychotherapy, an advertising campaign, a political speech, and a sermon share the general objectives of attempting to persuade and influence another person, and all rely on the same basic strategies:

- Appeals to authority
- Appeals to intelligence and logic
- Arousal and focusing of emotions
- Negotiation and bargaining
- Use of reward

These strategies are not equivalently effective and all carry some risk to the patient. Although they can all be used to some advantage, they are arranged here, roughly, in the order of the risks associated with their use.

For example, assertions of one's expertise, authority, and status as the only means of persuasion carry many particular dangers. A therapist who asserts her version of truth simply because of her "superior" authority, experience, or training is likely to appear arbitrary. Such appeals do not lend themselves to offering reasons or rationales for adopting the therapist's point of view, and assertions of truth from this self-viewed role as expert often sound dogmatic and one-sided. They are.

The assumption that the therapist's opinion should be respected and followed simply because he is the therapist is almost certain to ensure a bad experience. A self-identified expert, whether patient or therapist, invites both blind obedience and ignorant rebellion. Neither response does much to increase your ability, skill, or knowledge. Moreover, appeals to one's own authority, along with the strategy of negotiation and bargaining, are likely to deteriorate into a process of coercion and threat when the therapist is frustrated.

In contrast, appeals to the patient's sense of logic—intellectual appeals—as a method of persuasion imply at least a modicum of respect and regard for the patient's right of self-direction and implicitly acknowledge the patient's personal strengths and intellectual resources. However, this type of appeal often appears false. Appeals to logic also frequently convey the impression that the therapist is holding back certain knowledge that would be helpful if it were forthcoming. Instead, the therapist seems to be asking the patient to reach the same conclusion that the therapist has reached. The process can degenerate into a guessing game, in which the patient becomes so concerned about discovering the "secret knowledge" of the therapist, that personal exploration is forgotten. This implied search for the therapist's version of truth can interrupt the egalitarian nature of the relationship and create an environment of gamesmanship and contentiousness.

Arousal and focusing of emotions, the third method of exercising influence, also may give rise to fear, defensiveness, and avoidance. A patient must be very motivated to withstand some of the emotional intensity stimulated by these procedures. A therapist not acutely tuned to your emotional state may misjudge how much emotional stress you can tolerate before losing heart and abandoning ship. If the therapist overestimates your level of tolerance, reversals may occur. You may become sensitized to fearful events rather than desensitized and more tolerant of stress.

Negotiation and bargaining, like appeals to therapist authority and status, may deteriorate into a contest of who is most important, knowledgeable, or skillful. While therapists who use negotiation have the opportunity to restore a patient's sense of power and control, the results mean an even more disastrous loss of self-esteem and self-confidence if this process goes awry.

Application of reward, through the processes of acknowledgment, support, encouragement, and praise, is the last and least risky of the persuasion tactics available to the psychotherapist. Indeed, any treatment that does not include some reward and acknowledgment from the therapist is, at best, unable to capitalize on the motivating power of acceptance. At worst, such a therapy will be one of criticism and implied criticism.

But, even reward and encouragement can be taken too far if they exceed the therapist's level of credibility. Praise and reward must be gauged to fit with patient levels of acceptance and tolerance to be effective. You cannot and should not deny your own best judgment, and the assessment of improvement must include how your feelings and impressions have changed. To make these appraisals, you must have knowledge.

There are three sequential and essential tests of your progress.

The first is a determination of *whether you are able to establish a meaningful and effective working relationship with your therapist.* This is purely subjective. This test can come as early as the third session, and may be the only test you employ while shopping for a therapist who can help. There is no substitute for trying out a therapist to find out if that person has the qualities that will help you bring about change in your life. Do the two of you click? Do you communicate? Do you feel supported and helped?

Don't reject impressions because they are subjective. You must ask yourself if you are being helped, and if the therapist excites your cooperation or your defenses. If you feel accepted, cared for, respected, and heard, this first test is passed.

Just as positive feelings about your therapist are good signs, there also are early indications that a therapist may lack the technical or personal skill to be of help. You may need to ask your therapist about certain aspects of her approach to make some of these determinations, however. Specifically, you should raise concerns about boundary violations if certain key events occur.

- The therapist spends time talking about his problems
- The therapist asks you for favors
- The therapist departs from standard procedures in setting your fees, arranging your appointments, and offering favors
- The therapist attempts to establish a personal relationship with you outside the office

These signs of boundary violations may not be problematic, but each increases the risk, allowing the therapist to lose objectivity and perspective. However, if you have questions about the appropriateness of the therapist's behavior, you may seek another clinician's opinion.

Certain practices also indicate that what the therapist is doing won't develop and facilitate a meaningful and helpful relationship. Concern should be raised:

- If the therapist blames and criticizes you for your problems
- If the therapist makes fun of you or frequently becomes angry and defensive
- If the therapist responds to your concerns by blaming you and insisting (not just suggesting) that her interpretation of events is more accurate than yours
- If the therapist tries to convince you that certain things happened to you in your life that you can't remember

The second test of your progress lies in an *assessment of how much your symptoms change.* Changes in the severity and pattern of problems that motivated you to seek treatment take a bit longer than the formation of a working relationship. The symptoms of about 50 percent of patients are alleviated within a four-month period, and about 80 percent of people experience relief within a year. Longer treatments affect basic coping styles and need systems, and are often required if your problem is long-standing, manifested in many ways, and complex.

Though we cannot expect most symptoms to be gone within a period of two or three months, this is a sufficiently long time to determine if there is movement in the right direction. You should begin to notice some change in the patterns, frequency, or intensity of symptoms within this span.

Don't rely on your memory to evaluate whether your symptoms change. To make a meaningful assessment of change, it is helpful to keep a diary or journal. Some therapists will ask you to fill out a symptom rating form on a regular basis. Copies will help you recall your progress.

Keep these records from the time of your first appointment. They will serve as an external check, and you can use them as points of reference for assessing how your symptoms have changed. If you don't have records, you might talk with those who have known you throughout the period. Recruit them to help you assess your changes.

However, even your friends' ratings are subject to bias. They may be afraid of hurting your feelings or they may have poor memories. To make the process yield a more reliable and useful index of your status, a little structure in the ratings is useful. We recommend a procedure borrowed from studies of addictive behavior—a method of assisted recall.

For this procedure, you will need a calendar of the three-month period before which you began treatment, another calendar of the most current month, a twelve-inch ruler, as well as some graph paper. Then follow these steps:

1. Identify key dates on each of the calendars. Label dates such as birthdays, weddings, holidays, special personal events, and vacations.
2. Engage your friends or family members in a process of trying to recall all the activities that brought you together around any of these dates. Have your friends recall, in as much detail as possible, both your actions and their impressions of you.
3. Each of you should independently rate the severity of your prob-

lems around each of the targeted dates by marking a place on the ruler. Identify one end of the ruler as the most severe and the other as no symptoms or problems on a scale of one to twelve. Write down the numbers of your ratings; do not reveal your ratings to your friends until they are complete.

4. Draw a graph representing the change in the ratings during the three months before treatment and the months since beginning treatment. If the slope of at least half the lines is not downward, bring the matter up with your therapist. At that point, it is time to consider the third test of progress.

If you have determined that your symptoms and problems have continued at the same rate, frequency, and severity as when you first entered treatment, it is time to reconsider whether you are receiving the kind of care you have a right to expect. If you sought help with your depression, you should be less depressed or depressed less frequently than you were before. If you are not, then it is time for the third test.

In the third test of progress, *question the scientific foundations of the therapist's practices and assumptions.* This is the level at which you can decide if the therapist is using procedures that have a maximum likelihood of success.

At this level, it will be necessary for you to ask your therapist for a description of her treatment rationale and references to published research on the effectiveness of the treatment being provided. Ethical and responsible therapists will respect and honor this request without offense. The ignorant therapist, the malicious therapist, the misdirected therapist, and the incompetent therapist won't.

Any concerns you have with these issues should be an opening to ask for an external review of your progress by a disinterested clinician, and should be used as an opening to talk to your therapist about a transfer to another therapist.

Remember, each therapist's approach reflects both personal theories and professional or working models of change. Because of this:

- Your progress will be greater if the therapist's philosophy of treatment, goals, and methods is compatible with your philosophy and perspective on life.

- You have a right to find out what your therapist's philosophy and beliefs are so that you can decide if you want to continue to work in such a framework.
- The more specific either the symptoms or causes of your difficulties, and the more debilitating the problems, the more relevant the particular training and experience of your therapist and the more important it is that you get specific kinds of treatment. It is also of greater benefit, in this latter case, that the treatments used are founded on good scientific research.

Fundamentally, the objectivity of science remains the greatest protection both to you and your psychotherapist during those times when treatment is not going well. Mental health and behavioral science offer an objective way of determining what procedures and methods are most likely to provide relief of symptoms and distress. A therapist needs this information to offer the best treatment available. If you are progressing at a rate that satisfies you, you haven't got a problem. If you are not making as much progress as you think you should, you need to know what works to ensure that you're getting the best treatment available. In Chapter 8, we offered a description of the primary treatments for some of the problems that trouble most people. Use this guide and do your own library research to identify other treatments and methods that can be the basis for discussion with your therapist.

It may be difficult for you to get direct and reliable information about scientifically established treatments for the particular problems you are experiencing. It may be necessary to supplement your research with a second opinion from another therapist of your choice. All your findings and concerns should be used as an opportunity to ask questions of your therapist and garner more knowledge about the scientific basis for your treatment.

We know that the process of seeking and benefiting from mental health treatment is difficult, and made all the more so by the foolishness that often passes for good therapy. But the effort is worth the price.

We encourage you, and hope you take an active role in your pursuit of self-understanding.

Appendix

American Psychological Association
    750 First Street NE; Washington, DC 20002-4242;
    (202) 336-5500.

American Board of Professional Psychology
    2100 East Broadway; Suite 313; Columbia, MO 65201;
    (314) 875-1267.

Association of State and Provincial Psychology Boards
    400 South Union; Montgomery, AL 36104.

American Psychiatric Association
    1400 K Street NW; Washington DC 20005;
    (202) 682-6000.

American Board of Psychiatry and Neurology
    500 Lake Cook Road; Suite 335; Deerfield, IL 60015.

National Association of Social Workers
    750 First Street NE; Suite 700; Washington DC 20002-4241;
    (202) 408-8600.

American Association of State Social Work Boards
    400 South Ridge Parkway; Suite B; Culpeper, VA 22701;
    (203) 829-6880.

American Psychiatric Nurses Association
    1200 19th Street NW; Suite 300; Washington, DC 20036;
    (202) 857-1133.

American Association of Marriage, Family, and Child Therapy
    1133 15th Street NW; Suite 300; Washington, DC 20005;
    (202) 452-0109.

Suggested Readings

CHAPTER 1

Beutler, L. E., Machado, P. P. P., & Neufeldt, S. (1994). Therapist variables. In S. L. Garfield & A. E. Bergin (Eds.), *Handbook of Psychotherapy and Behavior Change*, 4th ed. (pp. 259–269). New York: Wiley.

Beutler, L. E., Williams, R. E., & Wakefield, P. J. (1993). Obstacles to disseminating applied psychological science. *Journal of Applied and Preventive Psychology*, 2, 53–58.

Beutler, L. E. & Kendal, P. C. (Eds.) (Special Section Editors) (1995). The case for training in the provision of psychological therapy. *Journal of Consulting and Clinical Psychology*, 63, 179–213.

Beutler, L. E., Williams, R. E., Wakefield, P. J., & Entwistle, S. R. (1995). Bridging scientist and practitioner perspectives in clinical psychology. *American Psychologist*, 50, 984–994.

Bongar, B. & Beutler, L. E. (Eds.) (1995). *Comprehensive Textbook of Psychotherapy: Theory and Practice*. New York: Oxford Unversity Press.

Garfield, S. L. (1994). Research on client variables in psychotherapy. In A. E. Bergin & S. L. Garfield (Eds.), *Handbook of Psychotherapy and Behavior Change*, 4th ed. (pp. 190–228). New York: Wiley.

Howard, K. I., Kopta, S., Krause, M., & Orlinsky, D. (1986). The dose-effect relationship in psychotherapy. *American Psychologist*, 41, 159–164.

Jacobson, N. S. (1995). The overselling of therapy. *Networker*, March, 41–47.

Kazdin, A. E. (1986). The evaluation of psychotherapy: Research design and methodology. In S. L. Garfield & A. E. Bergin (Eds.), *Handbook of Psychotherapy and Behavior Change*, 3rd ed. (pp. 23–68). New York: Wiley.

Luborsky, L., Barber, J. P., & Beutler, L. E. (Special Section Editors.) (1993). Curative factors in dynamic psychotherapy. *Journal of Consulting and Clinical Psychology*, 61, 539–610.

CHAPTER 2

Bergin, A. E. & Lambert, M. J. (1978). The evaluation of psychotherapeutic outcomes. In S. L. Garfield & A. E. Bergin (Eds.), *Handbook of Psychotherapy and Behavior Change: An Empirical Analysis* 2d ed. (pp. 139–190). New York: Wiley.

Christensen, A. & Jacobson, N. S. (1994). Who (or what) can do psychotherapy: The status and challenge of nonprofessional therapies. *Psychological Science*, 5 (1), 8–14.

Evans, M. D., Hollon, S. D., De Rubeis, R. J., Piasecki, J. M., Grove, W. M., Garvey, M. J., & Tauson, V. B. (1992). Differential relapse following cognitive therapy and pharmacotherapy for depression. *Archives of General Psychiatry*, 49, 802–808.

Hollon, S. D., DeRubeis, R. J., Evans, M. D., Wiemer, M. J., Garvey, M. J., Grove, W. M., & Tauson, V. B. (1992). Cognitive therapy and pharmacotherapy for depression: Singly and in combination. *Archives of General Psychiatry*, 49, 774–781.

Lambert, M. J. (1991). An introduction to psychotherapy research. In L. E. Beutler and M. Crago (Eds.), *Psychotherapy Research: An International Review of Programatic Studies* (pp. 1–11). Washington, D.C.: American Psychological Association.

Lambert, M. J., Shapiro, D. A., & Bergin, A. E. (1986). The effectiveness of psychotherapy. In S. L. Garfield & A. E. Bergin (Eds.), *Handbook of Psychotherapy and Behavior Change*, 3rd ed. (pp. 157–211). New York: Wiley.

Seligman, M. E. P. (1995). The effectiveness of psychotherapy: The Consumer Reports study. *American Psychologist*, 50, 965–974.

Smith, M. L., Glass, G. V., & Miller, T. I. (1980). *The Benefits of Psychotherapy*. Baltimore: The Johns Hopkins University Press.

Staff (1995). Mental health: Does therapy help? *Consumer Reports*, November, 734–739.

CHAPTER 3

Aaron, H. (1996). End of an era. *The Brookings Review*, 14 (1), 35–37.

Barlow, D. H., Hayes, S. C., & Nelson, R. O. (1984). *The Scientist Practitioner: Research and Accountability in Clinical and Educational Settings*. New York: Pergamon Press.

Beutler, L. E., Kim, E. J., Davison, E., Karno, M., & Fisher, D. (1996). Research contributions to improving mental health care outcomes. *Psychotherapy*, 33, 197–206.

Luborsky, L., McLellan, T., Woody, G. E., O'Brien, C. P., & Auerbach, A. (1985). Therapist success and its determinants. *Archives of General Psychiatry*, 42, 602–611.

Mahoney, M. J. (1991). *Human Change Processes: The Scientific Foundations of Psychotherapy*. New York: Basic Books.

Sperry, L., Brill, P. L., Howard, K. I., & Grissom, G. R. (1996). *Treatment Outcomes in Psychotherapy and Psychiatric Interventions*. New York: Brunner/Mazel.

Stein, D. M. & Lambert, M. J. (1995). Graduate training in psychotherapy: Are therapy outcomes enhanced? *Journal of Consulting and Clinical Psychology*, 63, 182–196.

Strupp, H. H., Hadley, S. W., & Gomes-Schwartz, B. (1997). *Psychotherapy for Better or Worse: The Problem of Negative Effects*. New York: Jason Aronson.

CHAPTER 4

American Psychiatric Association (1995). *Opinions of the Ethics Committee on the Principles of Medical Ethics*. Washington, D.C.: American Psychiatric Press.

American Psychological Association (1992). Ethical principles of psychologists and code of conduct. *American Psychologist*, 47, 1597–1611.

Beutler, L. E. (1995). The germ theory myth and the myth of outcome homogeneity. *Psychotherapy* (Special Section), 32, 489–494.

Beutler, L. E. & Harwood, T. M. (1995). Prescriptive psychotherapies. *Applied and Preventive Psychology*, 4, 89–100.

Epstein, R. S. (1994). *Keeping Boundaries: Maintaining Safety and Integrity in the Psychotherapeutic Process*. Washington, D.C.: American Psychiatric Press.

Orlinsky, D. E., Grawe, K., & Parks, B. K. (1994). Process and outcome in psychotherapy—Noch Einmal. In A. E. Bergin and S. L. Garfield

(Eds.), *Handbook of Psychotherapy and Behavior Change*, 4th ed. (pp. 270–376). New York: Wiley.

Orlinsky, D. E. & Howard, K. I. (1986). Process and outcome in psychotherapy. In S. L. Garfield & A. E. Bergin (Eds.), *Handbook of Psychotherapy and Behavior Change*, 3rd ed. (pp. 311–384). New York: Wiley.

Pope, K. S. (1991). Dual relationships in psychotherapy. *Ethics and Behavior*, 1, 21–34.

CHAPTER 5

Beutler, L. E. (1989). Differential treatments selection: The role of diagnosis in psychotherapy. *Psychotherapy*, 26, 271–281.

Follette, W. C. & Houts, A. C. (1996). Models of scientific progress and the role of theory in taxonomy development: A case study of the DSM. *Journal of Consulting and Clinical Psychology*.

Good, B. J. (1993). Culture, diagnosis and comorbidity. *Culture, Medicine and Psychiatry*, 16, 427–446.

Hadley, S. W. & Autry, J. H. (1984). DSM-III and psychotherapy. In S. Turner & Hersen (Eds.), *Adult Psychopathology and Diagnosis* (pp. 465–484). New York: Wiley.

Hayes, S. C., Wilson, K. G., Gifford, E. V., & Follette, W. C. (1996). Experiential avoidance and behavioral disorders: A fundamental dimensional approach to diagnosis and treatment. *Journal of Consulting and Clinical Psychology*, 16.

Morey, L. & McNamara, T. P. (1987). Comments: On definitions, diagnosis and DSM-III. *Journal of Abnormal Psychology*, 96, 283–285.

Schulberg, H. C. & McClelland, M. (1987). Depression and physical illness: The prevalence, causation, and diagnosis of comorbidity. *Clinical Psychology Review*, 7, 145–167.

CHAPTER 6

Bongar, B. & Beutler, L. E. (Eds.) (1995). *Comprehensive Textbook of Psychotherapy: Theory and Practice*. New York: Oxford University Press.

Freedheim, D. K. (Ed.) (1992). *History of Psychotherapy*. Washington, D.C.: American Psychological Association.

Patterson, C. H. & Watkins, C. E. Jr. (1996). *Theories of Psychotherapy*, 5th ed. New York: HarperCollins.

Reichenbach, H. (1964). *The Rise of Scientific Philosophy*. Berkeley: University of California Press.

Safran, J. D. & Greenberg, L. S. (Eds.) (1991). *Emotion, Psychotherapy and Change*. New York: Guilford Press.

Seligman, M. E. P. (1994). *What You Can Change and What You Can't*. New York: Knopf.

CHAPTER 7

Barlow, D. H., Hayes, S. C., & Nelson, R. O. (1984). *The Scientist Practitioner: Research and Accountability in Clinical and Educational Settings*. New York: Pergamon Press.

Beutler, L. E. (1991). Have all won and must all have prizes? Revisiting Luborsky, et al.'s verdict. *Jounal of Consulting and Clinical Psychology*, 59, 226–232.

Task Force on Promotion and Dissemination of Psychological Procedures (1995). Training in and dissemination of empirically validated treatments: Report and recommendations. *The Clinical Psychologist*, 48 (1), 3–23.

CHAPTER 8

Chambless, D. L., Sanderson, W. C., Shoham, V., Johnson, S. B., Pope, K. S., Crits-Christoph, P., Baker, M., Johnson, B., Woody, S. R., Sue, S., Beutler, L. E., Williams, D. A., & McCurry, S. (1996). An update on empirically validated therapies. *The Clinical Psychologist*, 49 (2), 5–14.

Bellack, A. S. & Hersen, M. (Eds.) (1990). *Handbook of Comparative Treatments for Adult Disorders*. New York: Wiley.

Kazdin, A. E. (1980). *Research Designs in Clinical Psychology*. New York: Harper and Row.

Smith, M. L., Glass, G. V., & Miller, T. J. (1980). *The Benefits of Psychotherapy*. Baltimore. The Johns Hopkins University Press.

CHAPTER 9

Beutler, L. E. & Clarkin, E. (1990). *Systematic Treatment Selection: Toward Targeted Therapeutic Interventions*. New York: Brunner/Mazel.

Beutler, L. E. & Crago, M. (Eds.) (1991). *Psychotherapy Research: International Programatic Studies*. Washington, D.C.: American Psychological Association.

Borys, D. S. & Pope, K. S. (1980). Dual relationships between therapist and client: A rational study of psychologists, psychiatrists and social workers. *Professional Psychology: Research and Practice*, 20, 283–293.

Crits-Christoph, P., Baranackie, K., Kurcias, J. S., Beck, A. T., Carroll, K., Perry, K., Luborsky, L., McLellan, A. T., Woody, G. E., Thompson, L., Gallagher, D., Zitrin, C. (1991). Meta-analysis of therapist effects in psychotherapy outcome studies. *Psychotherapy Research I*, 81–91.

Peterson, M. (1992). *At Personal Risk: Boundary Violations in Professional Relationships*. New York: Norton.

Index

abandonment, as depression cause, 137
abuse(s)
  in childhood. *See* childhood abuse
  in mental health field, 6
  victims, hypnosis therapy of, 75
Academy of Child and Adolescent
  Psychiatry, 54
accountability
  managed health care and, 54–56
  in psychotherapy, 45–62
accrediting bodies, for universities and
  colleges, 50–51
acupuncture, for post-traumatic stress disorder, 151
addictions, 183–184
  psychotherapy for, 42, 184
  role in mental illness, 33, 88–91, 184
Adler, Alfred, 103
advertisements, of therapists, 29
African Americans, psychological problems of, 42
aggressive impulses, conflict from, 104,
  105
agoraphobia, treatment of, 156, 157, 158,
  159, 160
Aguarana people (Peru), suicide in, 92
alcohol
  negative effects on sleep, 170
  withdrawal from, 89
alcoholism
  in depressed persons, 72

genetic factors in, 114
  perceived cause of, 88
  in psychiatric patients, 29
  suicide from, 92
  therapy of, 42, 55
Alzheimer's disease
  disrupted neural circuitry in, 115
  symptoms of, 88
American Association of Marriage,
  Family, and Child Therapy,
  address of, 198
American Association of State Social
  Work Boards, address of, 197
American Board of Professional
  Psychology, address of, 197
American Board of Psychiatry and
  Neurology, address of, 197
American Medical Association, accrediting functions of, 51
American Psychiatric Association
  accrediting functions of, 51
  address of, 197
  diseases-of-the-mind lists of, 82, 83
  homosexuality reassessment by, 81
  membership directory of, 54
American Psychiatric Nurses Association,
  address of, 198
American Psychological Association
  (APA)
  accrediting functions of, 51
  address of, 197

(APA) (cont.)
  psychological procedure guidelines of,
    132–133
  psychotherapy model review by, 24
American Psychological Society, accrediting functions of, 51
anal developmental stage, 102
anecdotal evidence, reliance on, 15
anger, in patient-therapist relationship,
  68–69, 77
anorexia
  as life threatening, 166
  treatment of, 165, 168, 178
antidepressants, sleep improvement by, 170
anxiety. See also generalized anxiety disorder (GAD)
  acceptance of, 154–155
  biological therapy of, 176
  causes of, 116
  diagnosis of, 80, 136
  differential diagnosis of, 146, 147
  in eating disorders, 167
  forms of, 147
  medications for, 41
  psychotherapy for, 37, 38, 113,
    146–161, 175, 176
  requiring treatment, 4
apnea, 169
arousal and focusing of emotions, in psychotherapy, 190, 191–192
Asian Americans, psychological problems
  of, 42
Association of State and Provincial
  Psychology Boards,
  address of, 197
associations, use for credential checking,
  53, 61, 197–198
authority appeals, in psychotherapy, 190,
  191
auto accidents, post-traumatic stress disorder from, 149, 151
avoidance prevention, in anxiety therapy,
  146–147

"baby blues", after pregnancy, 3
behavior
  acceptable, social value determination
    of, 81
  biological models of, 99, 114–116
  causes of, 114
  cognitive-behavioral models of, 99,
    105–109, 138, 142–144
  humanistic-experimental models of, 99,
    109–112
  interpersonal-systems models of, 99,
    112–114
  psychodynamic models of, 99–105,
    111, 116
  theories of, 99
behavioral exchange, in marital discord
  therapy, 172
behavioral therapy, 97–98, 107, 175
  of chronic pain, 178
  of depression, 142–143, 175, 178
  of eating disorders, 165, 166–167, 178
  of headaches, 162
  of insomnia, 169–170, 178
  of marital discord, 172–173
  of obsessive-compulsive disorders, 178
  of panic attacks, 160, 178
  of phobias, 178
  of sexual dysfunction, 175, 178
behaviorism, in psychological therapy,
  105–109, 109
behavior problems, genetic aspects of, 90
Bergen-Belsen [Nazi death camp], 11
Bianchi, Ken [Hillside Strangler], 84
binge eating, treatment of, 165, 167
biofeedback
  for chronic pain treatment, 163
  for post-traumatic stress disorder, 151
Biographical Directory of the American
  Psychiatric Association, 54
biological models of behavior, 99,
  114–116
biological therapy, 175
  of depression, 137–138, 175, 178
  of obsessive-compulsive disorders, 175,
    178
  of post-traumatic stress disorder,
    149–150, 178
  of sleep disorders, 178
bipolar disorder
  diagnosis of, 80, 136
  genetic factors in, 114
  medication for, 93
  treatment of, 138
blind tests, 129
Board Certified, as award for passed competency examinations, 53
bodily secretions, role in behavior, 114
boundary violations, in psychotherapy,
  65–67, 186, 193
brain tumor, misdiagnosis of, 79

breach-of-trust case, in psychotherapy, 66
Breuer, Josef, 100
bulimia, treatment of, 165, 166–168, 178

calendar of key events, for patients,
    194–195
Carpenter, Karen, 166
Carroll, Lewis, 117
Certified Cognitive Therapist, 30
channel communications, by fraudulant
    psychologist, 46
chart, of psychotherapies, 178
chemical imbalance
    depression as possible, 12–13, 137
    role in mental illness, 88–91, 115
childhood abuse
    evidence of, 22–23
    group therapy for, 125–126
    perpetrators of, 22–23
    repressed memories of, 103, 148
    role in depression, 13, 21
chronic pain, treatment of, 161–165, 178
classical conditioning, 106
clergymen
    counseling provided by, 31, 43
    as source for reputable therapists, 60
clinical trials, randomized, 128
clinicians, designations of, 32, 33
Clinton, Bill, 18
cognitive-behavioral models, of behavior,
    99, 105–109
cognitive therapy, 63, 107, 108–109
    of chronic pain, 164–165
    of depression, 138, 139–143, 178
    of eating disorders, 166–167, 178
    of generalized anxiety disorder, 160
    of irritable bowel syndrome, 178
    of obsessive-compulsive disorders, 178
    of phobias, 178
    of post-traumatic stress disorder,
        150–152, 178
    of sexual dysfunction, 178
Committee on Accreditation (COA), func-
    tions of, 51
competence assessment, of psychothera-
    pists, 53
compulsions, definition of, 153
concentration camps, 11, 17
conditioning, in behaviorism, 105, 106
confidentiality breaches, by therapist, 78
Consumer Reports, psychotherapy survey
    in, 36, 38, 170

corrective emotional experience, as
    psychodynamic therapy, 104
counseling
    benefits of, 94
    psychotherapy compared to, 31, 32, 97
creativity, in psychotherapists, 75–77
credential checking, of psychotherapists,
    53, 61
criticism, by therapists, 69, 71, 77, 193
culture, disease and, 91–93
customary standard of the profession, role
    in legal cases, 59

death, as depression cause, 137
demographic factors, in choice of thera-
    pist, 44, 61
depersonalization
    of modern humanity, 110
    in post-traumatic stress disorder, 148,
        150
depression
    after pregnancy, 4
    behavioral therapy of, 138, 142–143,
        175, 178
    biological therapy of, 137–138, 175,
        178
    causes of, 12–14, 21, 88, 89–90, 116,
        140
    cognitive therapy of, 138, 139–142,
        178
    differential diagnosis of, 136, 146, 147
    in eating disorders, 40, 166, 168, 178
    interpersonal psychotherapy of, 142,
        143–144, 178
    medications for, 13, 40, 41, 138, 141,
        178
    patients' views of causes of, 18
    psychodynamic therapy of, 144–146,
        175, 178
    psychotherapy for, 4, 13, 37, 38, 72,
        113, 138–146, 176, 178(chart), 195
    relapses in, 38, 139
    repressed sexual abuse and, 13, 21
    self-limiting episodes of, 38
    suicide from, 92
    symptoms of, 72, 85, 86, 108,
        136–137, 139, 145, 168, 169
    vegetative signs of, 40
despair, feelings of, repressed sexual abuse
    and, 21
deviant behavior, medicalization of, 83,
    84–93

diagnosis(es)
  definition of, 94
  helpfulness of, 79–95
  in mental health, 80–81
  negative aspects of, 94
  uses and misuses of, 82–93
Diagnostic and Statistical Manual (DSM), 82, 83, 84
diagnostic labeling, illness and, 183–185
dieting, for eating disorders, 165
Diplomate, as award for passed competency examinations, 53–54, 61
directives and suggestions, from therapists, 69–70
directories, for psychotherapists, 54
disclosure doctrine, role in legal cases, 60
disease, culture and, 91–93
Doctor of Medicine (M.D.), as degree of psychiatrists, 26, 29, 33, 34, 75, 78
Doctor of Osteopathy (D.O.), as degree of psychiatrists, 26, 29, 33, 34
Doctor of Philosophy (Ph.D.), as degree of psychologists, 26, 29, 33, 34, 35, 75, 78
Doctor of Psychology (Psy.D.), as degree of psychologists, 26, 29, 33, 34, 35, 36
"Do No Harm" (Hippocratic oath), 6
dreams
  interpretation of, 100, 103, 104
  repressed sexual abuse and, 21
drug abuse
  behavioral problems following, 116
  therapy of, 55
drugs
  dependence on, 163
  testing of, 124
  use by middle classes, 35
dysfunctional behaviors, repression role in, 109

eating disorders, 161. *See also* anorexia; bulimia; obesity
  in depression, 40, 166, 168, 178
  types and treatment of, 165–168
eating patterns, cultural aspects of, 91
education, of mental health professionals, 4–5
effectiveness, of psychotherapy, 11–27, 36–39, 50–54, 62, 119–134, 193–194
ego, energy control by, 102
Einstein, Albert, 121
ejaculatory dysfunction, therapy for, 174–175

Elavil, 138
emotional abuse
  evidence of, 132
  post-traumatic stress disorder from, 149
emotionally focused therapy, of marital discord, 173
emotional problems
  culture role in, 92
  genetic aspects of, 90
  theories of, 114
energy changes, in depression, 40
environmental toxins, disrupted behavior from, 116
erectile dysfunction, therapy for, 174
ethnic groups, psychotherapy and, 42, 44
evil, persons perceived as, 84
existentialism, 110–111
experience, personal, role in psychotherapy efficacy, 16–27
experimental-humanistic therapy
  of chronic pain, 165
  of post-traumatic stress disorder, 152
experimental treatments, patient protection against, 59
expert witnesses, in malpractice suits, 59
eye movement desensitization, for anxiety and depression, 176

factual observations, validity of, 21–22
families
  support of, 43
  symptom bearer in, 112
family history, as part of initial evaluation, 131
fantasies, interpretation of, 014, 103
favors, from therapist, 65, 193
Federal Bureau of Investigation (FBI), 119
Fellow, as indication of advanced standing, 53, 61
female patients, sexual relationships with therapists, 64–65, 66–67
flashback memories, in post-traumatic stress disorder, 148
Flash Gordon, 185
flexibility, in psychotherapists, 75–77
Florida, malpractice in, 34
Food and Drug Administration (FDA), 24, 25, 58, 124
Frank, Jerome, 123
Frankl, Victor [Holocaust survivor], 110
Franklin, George, 181, 184

Franklin-Lipsker, Eileen, 181–182, 185–186

fraudulance, among psychotherapists, 46, 61

free-association method, in psychoanalysis, 103

Freud, Sigmund, 7, 183
psychoanalysis method of, 99–103

Gainji people (Papua New Guinea), suicide in, 92–93

Galileo, 121

generalized anxiety disorder (GAD), symptoms and treatment of, 160–161, 178

genetics
role in behavior, 114, 115
role in depression, 88

Gershwin, George, misdiagnosis of, 79

Gestalt Therapy Institute, 30

glucose, in blood, food deprivation and, 91

God, 120, 121, 122

grief process, role in psychotherapy, 46, 113

Group for the Advancement of Psychiatry, 54

group therapy, for abuse victims, 125–126

growth forces, in humanistic-experimental models of behavior, 110

gymnasts, as anorexics, 166

Hagelin, John, 18

Hal Roach Training Studio, 17

Hamlet, 127

happiness, as valued condition, 86

headaches
behavioral therapy of, 162
cognitive therapy of, 162
repressed sexual abuse and, 21

health care, U.S. costs of, 53, 54

heart palpitation, heart attack and, 16–17

Heidegger, Martin, 110

heights, fear of, repressed sexual abuse and, 21

Hillside Strangler [Ken Bianchi], 84

Hippocratic oath, 6

Hispanic Americans, psychological problems of, 42

Holocaust survivors
inner commitment of, 109–110

survivor's guilt in, 11

homework assignments
in cognitive therapy, 109, 140, 166
in depression therapy, 140
in eating disorder therapy, 166
in generalized anxiety disorder therapy, 160
in sexual dysfunction therapy, 174

homosexuality, American Psychiatric Association
classification of, 81, 82

Hood v. Phillips, 57

horse training, analogy to psychotherapy, 75–76

hostility, in psychotherapists, 69

humanistic-experimental models, of behavior, 99, 109–112

humanistic-experimental therapy, 175, 176, 178
of depression, 142, 176
of eating disorders, 178
of generalized anxiety disorder, 178
of obsessive-compulsive disorder, 155–156

Husserl, Edmund, 110

hyperventilation
heart attack and, 16–17
in panic attacks, 159

hypnosis
for chronic pain treatment, 163
memory recovery during, 181–182
for post-traumatic stress disorder, 151
use in therapy, 75, 100, 103

hysteria, self-cure of, 100

id, Freud's interpretation of, 100, 101, 102, 103

idiots, census classification of, 81

illnesses
diagnostic labeling and, 183–185
problems as, 33

imitation, behavior changing by, 107

informed consent doctrine, application to psychotherapy practive, 58–60

initial evaluation, in psychotherapy, 130–131

injury, behavioral problems following, 116

insane persons, census classification of, 81

insomnia, treatment of, 168–170

Institute of Science, Technology, and Public Policy, 18

institutional accountability, of psychotherapists, 50–54
insurance carriers, therapy payment by, 82, 94, 186–187
intellectual appeals, in psychotherapy, 190
interpersonal psychotherapy (IPT), 175
    of chronic pain, 178
    of depression, 142, 143–144, 178
    of eating disorders, 165, 178
    of obsessive-compulsive disorder, 155–156
    of sexual dysfunction, 178
interpersonal-systems models, of behavior, 99, 112–114
irritable bowel syndrome, symptoms and treatment of, 164, 178

Japan, suicide in, 93
Jesus Christ, 119, 120
job loss, as depression cause, 137
Johns Hopkins University, 123
Judeo-Christian heritage, suicide as sin in, 92
Jung, Carl, 103
Jungian Analyst, 30

Kierkegaard, Søren, 110
King, Steven, 19
knowledge, avenues of, 15

labels, negative aspects of, 94–95, 183–185
law
    psychotherapeutic efficacy and, 23
    psychotherapeutic malpractice and, 49, 57
Leach v. Braillar, 57
learning, in behaviorism, 105
legal cases
    involving managed health care, 56–57
    involving psychotherapy, 49, 57, 66
libido, 102
Licensed Clinical Social Workers (LCSW), 33
Licensed Practical Nurse (L.P.N.), 34
licensing boards, credential review by, 52–53
listening ability, importance in psychotherapy, 39–40
London, Ray, 7
Lorenz, Paul, 101

LSD, use by middle classes, 35

Maharishi Mahash Yogi, 18
malpractice, control of, 34–35
malpractice suits
    expert witnesses in, 59
    against psychotherapists, 49
managed health care, 183
    accountability vs. cost in, 54–56
    myths about psychotherapy in, 71–72, 73
    patient dissatisfaction with, 56
manic-depressive disorder, diagnosis of, 80, 136
marijuana, use by middle classes, 35
marital discord, therapy of, 171–173, 175, 176
mass media, reliance on single studies by, 128
Master of Arts (M.A.), 26, 34, 52
Master of Behavioral Counseling (M.B.C), 34, 35
Master of Education (M.Ed.), 34, 52
Master of Family and Child Counseling (M.F.C.C.), 26, 29, 34, 52
Master of Science (M.S.), 26, 34, 52
Master of Social Work (M.S.W.), 26, 29, 33, 40
medical history, as part of initial evaluation, 131
medical judgment, role in legal cases, 59
medications
    for agoraphobia, 156
    for anxiety, 41
    for chronic pain, 164, 178
    for depression, 13, 40, 41, 138, 141
    for headaches, 162
    for insomnia, 170
    for mental illness, 39, 113, 116
    overuse of, 40
    for panic attacks, 45
    for post-traumatic stress disorder, 150
    for schizophrenia, 94
    sleep disorders from, 168, 169
memory, of Holocaust survivor, 12
memory repression
    in murder case, 181
    possible symptoms of, 21
mental health
    contemporary theories in, 99–116
    diagnosis in, 80–81
    self-help books on, 8

mental health care
  insurance for, 54
  legal aspects of, 56–58
  managed programs for, 55
mental health professionals
  education of, 4–5
  licensing of, 34
mental illness
  culture role in, 92
  relapse in, 40
  social construction of, 81–84
mental status examination, 130
metaphor expansionitis, 183
migraine headaches, treatment of, 163
minority doctrine, 23–24
myths and legends, in psychotherapy, 32,
  42–43, 71–72, 185–187

narcolepsy, symptoms and treatment of,
  168–169
Nason, Susan, 181
National Association of Social Workers
  (NASW), 33
  accrediting functions of, 51, 53
  address of, 197
National Register of Health Service
  Providers, 54
Nature Law Party, John Hagelin as candidate for, 18
negotiation and bargaining, in psychotherapy, 190, 192
neurological structure changes, role in
  behavior, 114
neurosis, 83
  as Freudian diagnosis, 100, 101
neurotransmitters
  role in behavior, 114
  role in depression, 88
  role in mental illness, 115
Newton, Isaac, 121
The New Yorker, 79
nightmares, in post-traumatic stress disorder, 148

obesity, 165, 178
obsessive-compulsive disorders
  as anxiety type, 147
  treatment of, 153–156, 161, 178
oedipal conflict, of Freud, 101
open spaces, fear of, repressed sexual
  abuse and, 21
operant conditioning, 106–107

opiates, withdrawal from, 89, 184
oral developmental stage, 102
orgasmic dysfunction, therapy for,
  173–174

pain
  chronic. See chronic pain
  hypnosis therapy of, 75
panic attacks
  as anxiety type, 147
  medication for, 45
  psychotherapy for, 45–47, 97,
    158–160, 178
  symptoms of, 159
paranoia, diagnosis of, 80, 84
Parkinson's disease, 90
  disrupted neural circuitry in, 115
  symptoms of, 88
passivity, undesirable, in therapists, 68
past events
  therapist beliefs in, 20–21
  when not to trust, 28
patient
  expectations of, 129–133
  motivation in, 68
  relationship with therapist, 63–78,
    111–112, 117, 177, 192–193
  role in psychotherapy, 93–41, 135–136
Pavlov, Ivan, 105–106, 107
personal experience, role in psychotherapy efficacy, 15, 16–27
pessimism
  in depressed people, 18
  in therapists, 87
phallic developmental stage, 102
phobias, 146
  as anxiety type, 147
  conditioned, 106
  treatment of, 11, 12, 156–158, 161,
    178
phone calls, inappropriate, 64, 65
physical abuse
  evidence of, 132
  post-traumatic stress disorder from,
    149
physicians
  counseling provided by, 43
  as source for reputable therapists, 60
plastic tokens, use in marital discord therapy, 173
post-traumatic stress disorder (PTSD)
  as anxiety type, 147

(PTSD) (cont.)
  biological therapy of, 149–150, 178
  cognitive therapy of, 150–152, 178
  treatment of, 148–153, 155, 161
pregnancy, "baby blues" after, 3
professional qualifications, of psychotherapists, 48–54
progressive relaxation exercise, by therapist, 64
Prozac, 93, 138
psychiatrists
  inadequate number after World War II,
  33
  professional associations of, 54
  training of, 26, 36
psychic determinism, 101
psychoanalysis
  of depression, 142
  Freud's system of, 99–103
  psychodynamic derivatives of, 104
  sessions in, 103
psychoanalyst, 30
psychodynamic models of behavior,
  100–105, 111, 116, 117
psychodynamic therapy, 175, 178
  of chronic pain, 165
  of depression, 144–146, 178
  of marital discord, 171–172, 173, 175
  of obsessive-compulsive disorder,
  155–156
  of panic attacks, 160
  of post-traumatic stress disorder, 152
psychological illnesses, behaviors identified as, 82
psychologists
  fraudulant, 46
  malpractice among, 34–35
  professional list of, 54
  training of, 26, 33, 36, 61
psychology, as college subject, 35
psychosexual development, role in
  Freudian psychoanalysis, 102
psychotherapists
  confidentiality breaches by, 78
  counselors compared to, 31, 32
  criticism of, 6
  definition of, 32–36
  directives and suggestions from, 69–70
  effective characteristics of, 67–70
  encouraging characteristics of, 72–73
  experience and skill in, 61, 73–75
  flexibility and creativity in, 75–77

  fraudulant, 47, 61
  institutional accountability of, 50–54
  negative qualities in, 68, 69, 77, 78
  passivity in, 68
  patient relationship with, 63–78, 177
  professional qualifications of, 48–54,
  60
  selection of, 30–31, 41–42, 60–62, 177,
  188, 189
  sexual relationship with patients,
  64–65, 66–67, 78
  staff memberships of, 61
  treatment guidelines for, 123–125
  unethical or unscrupulous, 53, 63–65,
  66
psychotherapy
  accountability of, 45–62
  alternatives to, 9, 31
  boundary violations in, 65–67, 186,
  193
  breach-of-trust case in, 66
  chart of treatments in, 178
  criticism of, 6
  decision to use, 188–190
  effectiveness of, 11–27, 36–39, 50–54,
  62, 119–134, 193–194
  evaluation of, 193–194
  expectations of patients in, 129–133
  guidelines in, 132
  initial evaluation in, 130–131
  judgments in, 15
  long-term, 41, 43, 78
  myths and legends in, 32, 42–43,
  71–72
  number of sessions for, 37
  patient's role in, 11–44
  progress evaluation in, 190–196
  second opinions in, 28, 95, 134, 177,
  196
  setbacks in, 37
  short periods of, 25
  specialties in, 29
  strategies in, 190–191
  theories of, 23
  treatment guidelines in, 123–125
  treatment types in, 12, 97–118, 132,
  135–179, 196
Public Broadcasting System, program on
  satanic abuse therapy, 19, 20
purging. See bulimia

radical behavior therapist, 107–108

randomized clinical trials, 128
rape, post-traumatic stress disorder from, 149, 151
Raynor, P., 106
Reagan, Ronald, 17, 85
reasonable patient, role in legal cases, 60
record keeping
    in depression therapy, 140
    in generalized anxiety disorder therapy, 160
    in headache therapy, 162
    role in social learning therapy, 108
    in therapy evaluation, 194
re-exposure treatment, for post-traumatic stress disorder, 150, 152–153
Registered Nurse (R.N.), 34
reinforcerment, of behavior, 107
relapse, in mental illnesses, 40
relationship problems, therapy for, 63, 64, 171–175
relaxation
    for anxiety treatment, 146, 155, 157
    for headache treatment, 163
    in panic attack therapy, 159
    for post-traumatic stress disorder, 151
religious beliefs, of patient, 131
remoralization, in psychotherapy, 123
repression
    as attitude of hopelessness, 109
    of childhood abuse, 103, 148
research
    design of, 125–129
    as evidence of treatment efficacy, 22–27
    role in psychotherapeutic practice, 15
    on social problems, 85–86
    on therapist training, 74
respectable minority principle, law and, 56–58, 59
rewards, use in psychotherapy, 190, 192
Rice, Ann, 19
risk factors, for behavior, 114
Rogers, Carl, 111–112
Rokeach, Milton, 120
Rubin, Solomon [Holocaust survivor], 11–12

Sartre, Jean-Paul, 110
satanic abuse therapy, exposé on, 19, 20
schizophrenia, 86
    causes of, 88
    diagnosis of, 80, 84
    genetic factors in, 114

medication for, 93
suicide from, 92
Taraxein and, 90
science
    protective potential of, 187–188
    role in practice, 120–123
scientific research
    as avenue to knowledge, 15, 22–27
    basis of, 121–122
    as evidence of treatment efficacy, 22–27
scientist practitioners, mental health professionals as, 8
second opinions, in psychotherapy, 28, 95, 134, 177, 196
selfactualization, 110
self-esteem
    in depressed people, 18
    repressed sexual abuse and, 21
self-healing, in interpersonal therapy, 113
self-help books
    on mental health, 8
    use for phobia treatment, 157–158
session length, inappropriate, 65
sexist categories, of mental illness, 83
sexual abuse
    evidence of, 132
    hysteria and, 100
    post-traumatic stress disorder from, 149, 152
    recollections of, 21
    in supposed satanic cults, 19, 20
sexual anxiety, repressed sexual abuse and, 21
sexual desire
    changes in, in depression, 40, 85
    repressed sexual abuse and, 21
sexual developmental stage, 102
sexual dysfunction, therapy of, 173–175, 176, 178
sexual fantasies, in mental illness, 100, 101, 104
sexual functioning, of patient, 131
sexual groups, psychotherapy and, 42
sexual impulses, conflict from, 104, 105
sexual relationship, between patient and therapist, 64–65, 66–67, 78
Singer, Margaret, 84
Skinner, B. F., 98, 106–107
sleep disorders, 161
    in depression, 40, 85, 146
    in post-traumatic stress disorder, 148
    treatment of, 168–170, 176, 178

social history, as part of initial evaluation, 131
social interactions, role in depression therapy, 40, 140, 142
social learning theory, 107, 108
social networks, support of, 43
social phobias, treatment of, 157
social reward, behavior changing by, 107
social role transitions, in interpersonal therapy, 113
social values, as determinants of acceptable behavior, 81
social withdrawal
  in depression, 85, 108
  in post-traumatic stress disorder, 148
social workers, degrees and training of, 33, 61
specific risk, for mental illnesses, 114–115
staff memberships, of psychotherapists, 61
State Board of Psychologist Examiners, 46
stimulus generalization, 106
stress, physical reactions to, 161–170
stress-inoculation, use in generalized anxiety disorder therapy, 161
stroke, symptoms of, 88
suicide
  from depression, 137, 139, 140, 141
  as psychotherapeutic emergency, 7
  thoughts of, 120
  repressed sexual abuse and, 21
  in various cultures, 92
superego, Freud's interpretation of, 100
survivor's guilt, in Holocaust survivor, 11, 12
symptoms, description of, 131
symptom bearer, in families, 112
systematic desensitization, as phobia treatment, 11, 157

talking, about therapy, 69
Taraxein, schizophrenia and, 90
Task Force on Promotion and Dissemination of Psychological Procedures, of American Psychological Association, 132–133
therapists. See psychotherapists
therapy. See psychotherapy
thought-field therapy, for anxiety and depression, 176

tobacco
  negative effects on sleep, 170
  withdrawal from, 89
tranquilizers, use for panic attacks, 45, 97
Transcendental Meditation movement, 18
treatment mediators, 127
tricyclic antidepressants (TCAs), 138, 141
trust, role in patient-therapist relationship, 14

unhappiness, depression and, 137
U.S. Bureau of the Census, disordered behavior
  classification of, 81
U.S. Department of Education, regional accrediting bodies of, 50, 51
University of California (Berkeley), 84
unreality feelings, in post-traumatic stress disorder, 148
USSR, 86

Valium, 97
vegetative signs, of depression, 40
Verne, Jules, 185
Vietnam War, psychological effects on soldiers and families, 33
violence, proposed reduction by meditation, 18–19
voices, heard with "baby blues", 3, 4

war experiences, post-traumatic stress disorder from, 149
Watson, J. B., 106
weight gain or loss, repressed sexual abuse and, 21
Western society, suicide in, 92
witchery, satanic abuse therapy and, 19, 20
withdrawal, from abuse substances, 89, 184
women, orgasmic dysfunction in, 173–174
work activity changes, in depression, 40
World War II, psychological effects on soldiers and families, 33

Xanax, 45, 93, 98

Yellow Pages, mental health professionals listed in, 29, 47